Word 365 Essentials

WORD 365 ESSENTIALS - BOOKS 1 AND 2

M.L. HUMPHREY

SELECT TITLES BY M.L. HUMPHREY

WORD 365 ESSENTIALS
Word 365 for Beginners
Intermediate Word 365

EXCEL 365 ESSENTIALS
Excel 365 for Beginners
Intermediate Excel 365

102 Useful Excel 365 Functions

WORD ESSENTIALS
Word for Beginners
Intermediate Word

See mlhumphrey.com for more Microsoft Office titles

CONTENTS

Word 365 for Beginners

WORD 365 ESSENTIALS - BOOK 1

M.L. HUMPHREY

CONTENTS

Introduction

Microsoft Word is a staple in the modern business world. I spent twenty years working with a variety of organizations as both a regulator and consultant in the financial services industry and every single entity I interacted with used Word for their word processing. It was also ubiquitous at every school I attended.

And while there may be industries that default to using other programs or people may have started using newer programs that do the same thing but are free, Microsoft Word is still the go-to program to learn for drafting documents.

I wrote the original *Word for Beginners* using Word 2013 to introduce users of any version of Microsoft Office to the core skills you need to use Word. That book is still a valid introduction to Word that any user could use today to get started.

But in the five years since that book was published, Microsoft has released newer versions of Word. And, of course, Word 365, which this book covers, is the constantly-evolving, most-recent, latest and greatest version of Word. Those new versions have changed the appearance of Word, which is why I wanted to publish this book with updated screenshots.

I am writing this book in January 2023 and for our purposes—a basic introduction to the core functions of Microsoft Word—you should be able to use this book for years to come and not have a problem. The basic functionality of Word does not change much. If anything, they add more bells and whistles to Word, they don't take them away.

Our focus in this book is going to be limited to just what you need to know to get started. The problem with the Microsoft Office programs is that they're so powerful that sometimes it can be overwhelming for a new user to learn what they need to know without getting bogged down in a lot of extraneous information they don't need. So we're going to focus in.

What are we going to cover?

I am going to start you off with the absolute basics of opening, saving, closing, deleting, and renaming a file. Then we'll cover how to add, delete, and move text in a Word document.

Next, we'll cover how to format that text at both the word and paragraph levels, including the use of basic bulleted and numbered lists.

We'll also cover find and replace, spelling and grammar check, and how to get a word count as well as how to add basic headers and footers, including page numbers, and also how to do some document-level formatting.

Finally, we'll cover how to print and customize your settings.

By the time we're done here you'll know about 90% of what you need to know to use Word on a daily basis, maybe more. I am not covering topics like track changes and tables, which you may also need, but which are also more complicated topics that I consider intermediate-level. They are covered in the next book in this series, *Intermediate Word 365*.

You don't have to continue to that book. I will give you in this book a strong foundation to build from when you're ready to add those other areas to your knowledge. Word has a great Help function you can use, and there are also numerous online resources out there.

Okay, then. Let's get started with a discussion of Office Themes so we can make sure that your screen looks like my screenshots.

Screenshots and Office Theme

Some of you who are brand new to Word may not be ready to change your Office Theme yet, because you don't know how to open a Word file and aren't familiar with the terminology I'm going to use, so will need to come back to this chapter later.

But for the rest of you, I wanted to cover this before you see your first set of screenshots so that we can all be on the same page.

As I mentioned above, one of the reasons I'm publishing this book rather than just letting everybody use *Word for Beginners,* which is still a perfectly adequate introduction to Word, is that the appearance of Microsoft Word changed with the release of Word 2021. And it changed enough to be noticeable.

I wanted to publish a book that had updated screenshots for users of Word 2021 or Word 365. But within Microsoft Office there are a number of "themes" that you can choose from that will impact the appearance of your document, so my screenshots still may not look the same as your version of Word.

Which is why, before we start I wanted to show you what I'm using for the rest of the book so that you can change those settings to match mine if that is important to you.

Okay, then. Here goes.

When I open Microsoft Word, I have the option to click on Account in the bottom left corner to go to the Account screen:

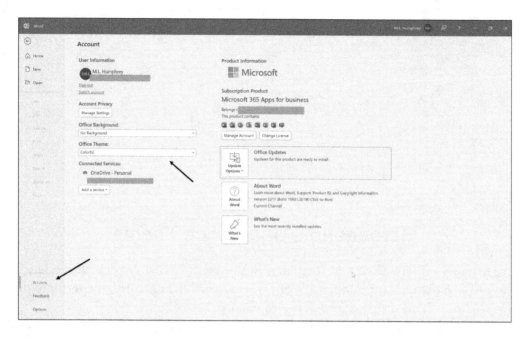

That screen has a dropdown that is labeled Office Theme. As you can see here, my theme is currently set to the Colorful theme. And that's the theme I will use for the rest of the book.

Here is an example of what the top left corner of a new document looks like using that theme:

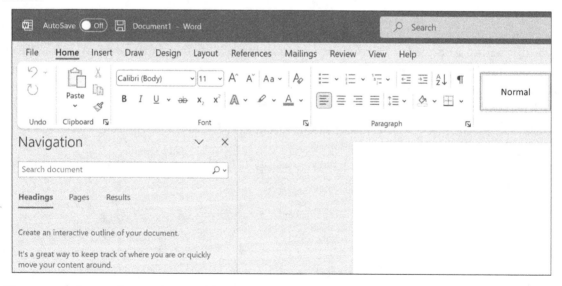

The top of the workspace in Word is colored blue. In Excel it's green. I assume in PowerPoint it's orange and in Access it's red. Most of the text is black and the background is a fairly light gray. The main document where you type is white.

Most of the screenshots I use in this book will not include that top bar, so if you're using the White theme, it will look much the same. Here that one is:

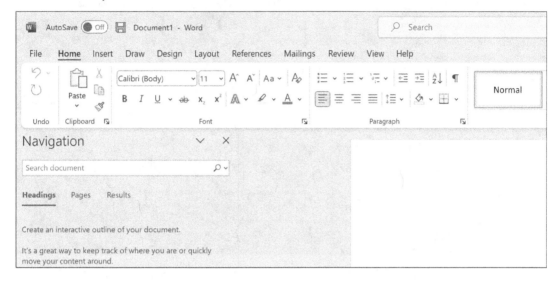

Note that the bar across the top is that light gray instead of blue, but for the most part the rest of it looks the same.

Where there can be bigger differences are with the Dark Gray and Black themes. Here is Dark Gray:

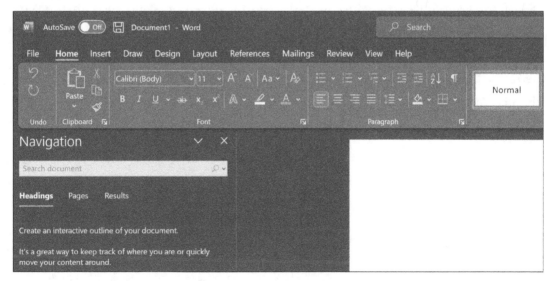

See that the background color is now a dark gray instead of a light gray and that the text is now white instead of black. But the main document is still white.

Here is the Black theme:

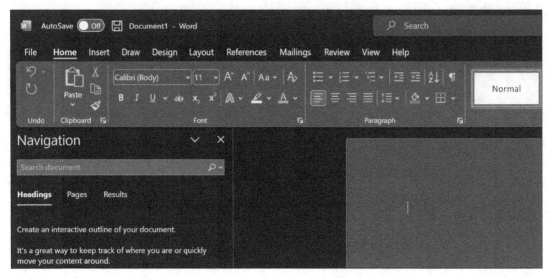

The background is now black. The text is white. But note that the main document where you'd type text is now a dark gray.

For most of what we do, those differences won't matter, but I wanted you to know about them because for me, for example, the difference between the Colorful or White themes and the Black theme are enough to be disconcerting. It throws me off to look at the Black theme.

So. If you want to have the same appearance as my screenshots and know that the colors I reference for dropdown items, etc. are the same, be sure to use the Colorful theme option. If you don't care, don't worry about it.

Also, another way to change this is to click on Options in that bottom left corner to open the Word Options dialogue box. You can change the Office Theme in the General section under Personalize Your Copy of Microsoft Office.

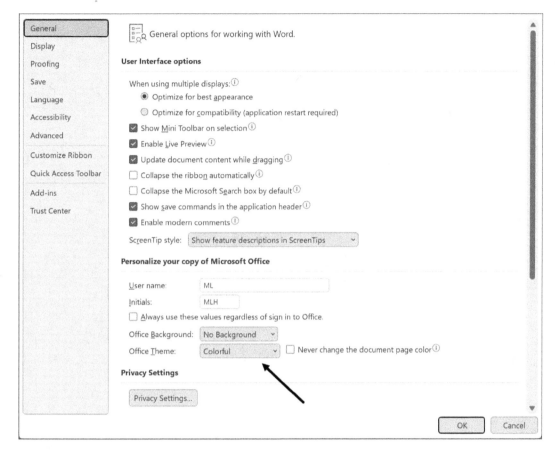

Note that any change you make to the theme applies to all Office programs, not just Word.

If your appearance still doesn't match mine it may be due to your computer's appearance settings which can also impact how Word appears on the screen.

Alright, now let's cover basic terminology so that we're all on the same page.

Basic Terminology

Most of these terms are used by everyone who uses Word, but a few may be my own quirk, so even if you're familiar with Word, please be sure to skim through.

Tab

When I refer to a tab in Microsoft Word, I will be referring to the menu options at the top of the screen. In older versions of Word when a menu option was selected it had the appearance of an old-time file tab, hence the name. But in the latest version of Word (Word 365 as of January 2023) they removed that. Now when a tab is selected, it's just underlined as you can see here with the Home tab.

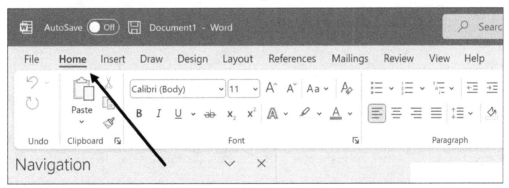

The other tab options that are available by default are File, Home, Insert, Draw, Design, Layout, References, Mailings, Review, View, and Help.

Each tab you select will show you different options or tasks. As you can see above, the Home tab allows you to Redo/Undo, Paste/Copy/Cut/Format Sweep, apply Font settings, apply Paragraph settings, and more. (We'll cover most of the Home tab in this book.)

Click

If I tell you to click on something, that means to move your cursor over to that location and then either right-click or left-click. If I don't say which to do, left-click.

Left-Click / Right-Click

If you look at a standard mouse, it's divided into two sides. Press down on the left side and that's a left-click. Press down on the right side and that's a right-click. You can also left- and right-click using your laptop's trackpad, but it won't always be obvious where to click. Usually it will be in the bottom of the trackpad. Pushing on the bottom left will left-click. Pushing on the bottom right will right-click.

A left-click is generally for selecting something. A right-click is generally for opening a dropdown menu.

Left-Click and Drag

If I ever tell you to left-click and drag, that means to left-click and then hold that left-click as you move your cursor. This is one way, for example, to select a range of text. You left-click at one end of the text and then hold that left-click as you move your mouse until all of the text you want is selected. It can also be a way to move an object.

Select or Highlight

There will be times when I tell you to select a range of text. Like here where I've selected the words "sample text":

This is sample text and I've selected the words that say that

When text is selected it will be highlighted or shaded a different color. In my Office theme, it is shaded a light gray.

As I noted above, one way to select text is to left-click and drag. You can left-click at either end of the range of text you want to select and then hold that left-click and drag your mouse until all of it is highlighted in gray.

Another option is to click at one end of the text, hold down the Shift key and use the arrow keys to select your text. The right and left arrows will move one character space at a time. The up and down arrows will move one row of text at a time.

If you need to select text that is not touching, you can do so using the Ctrl key. Select your first range of text, then hold down Ctrl while you left-click and drag to select your next range of text. (Using the arrow keys does not work. It will remove the first text selection.)

To select all of the text in a document you can use Ctrl + A.

Dropdown Menu

A dropdown menu is a list of choices. There are many dropdown menus in Word. One of the main ones is in the main workspace. Right-click on your document and you should see a dropdown menu that looks like this:

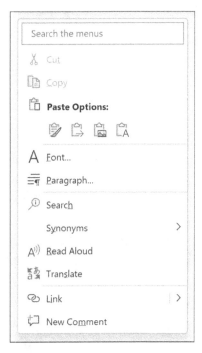

You can then select any of those choices from that dropdown to perform that task. Some dropdowns, like Synonyms, have a secondary dropdown menu. Hold your mouse over that arrow to the right of the option and you'll see another dropdown menu:

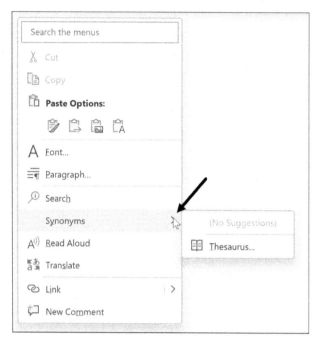

Many of the options in the tabs at the top of the workspace also have dropdown menus. They are indicated by an arrow either to the right of the option or below it. Here, for example, is the Font Color dropdown menu that you can see because I clicked on the arrow next to the red capital A.

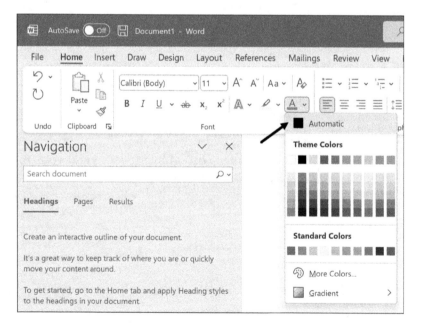

There is also a dropdown arrow under the Paste option on the left-hand side, as well as the underline, change case, text effects, bullets, numbering, and multi-level lists dropdowns that are visible in that screenshot.

(Don't worry if you don't know which is which, we'll cover most of them later.)

Expansion Arrow

The tasks under each tab are divided into different sections. So above you can see the Undo, Clipboard, Font, and Paragraph sections of the Home tab.

In the bottom right corner of most of those sections you will see an arrow. That's what I refer to as an expansion arrow. Click on that to see more options. Often it will open a dialogue box. (Which we'll define next.)

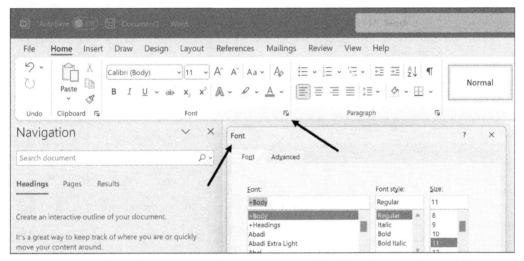

Here you can see that I clicked on the expansion arrow for the Font section and it opened the Font dialogue box.

Clicking on an expansion arrow is often the way to see the largest number of options, although I find I rarely need to do that.

Dialogue Box

Here is the full Font dialogue box that opened above:

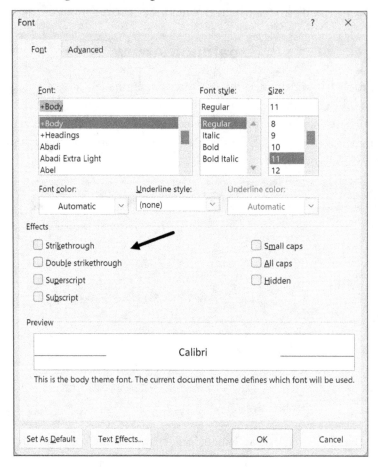

A dialogue box is a pop-up box that will open on top of your workspace and will usually include the largest number of choices for that particular setting or task. For example, here you can see that for Effects there are choices for strikethrough and double strikethrough. In the Home tab we only had the choice for strikethrough.

So if there's ever anything you want to do that you think should be possible, try opening a dialogue box to see if that option is listed.

To close a dialogue box, click on OK after you've made your selection or click on the X in the top right corner.

If you have more than one Word document open, you may need to close any open dialogue box before you can move between documents.

Scroll Bar

Once you have more text in your document than will fit on the screen, you will see scroll bars appear. In Word they usually are on the right-hand side. If you have your workspace zoomed to a level that won't show all of the text across a line, then you'll also see a scroll bar along the bottom. Like you can see here where the arrows point to the scroll bars, one on the top right, one along the bottom:

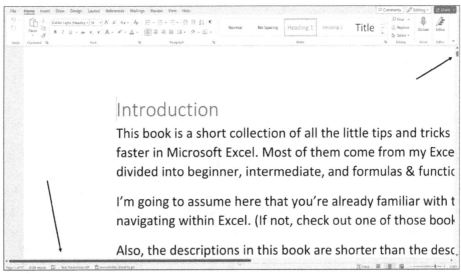

Note that the scroll bars are different sizes. The more text that isn't visible, the smaller the scroll bar will be.

Scroll bars may on occasion not be visible, but if you move your mouse over your document or over the edges where they should be located, they will reappear.

You can move through the document using the scrollbars in a number of ways. Left-click and drag the bar itself to flow through the document. Click in the lighter gray area at either end of the scroll bar to move one screen's worth of space. Left-click once on the arrows at the ends of the scroll bars to move about a line's worth of space. Or left-click and hold on those arrows to scroll through by about one line's worth of space at a time.

Scroll bars also appear for long lists of options where not all options fit on the screen. For example, the Font dropdown menu has a scroll bar on the right-hand side.

Task Pane

I believe by default you should have at least one task pane visible in your workspace for a new Word document. I do and I don't think I changed that setting. If so, it will be the Navigation task pane and be visible on the left-hand side of your workspace. Like so:

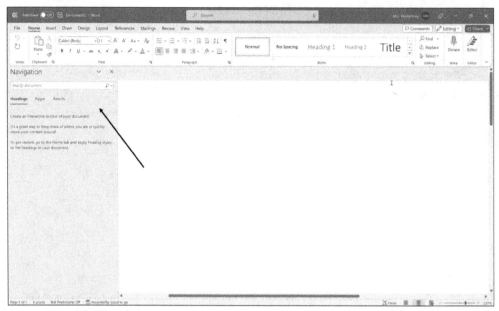

Task panes are a bit like dialogue boxes because they give you more options, but usually they will appear as part of your workspace, not on top of it like dialogue boxes do. Dialogue boxes are the old-school way of giving you more options. Task panes are the newer way of doing so. Which means for what we're doing in this book most of what you'll see are dialogue boxes.

You can open another task pane by going to the Help tab and clicking on Help, which will open the Help task pane on the right-hand side of your workspace.

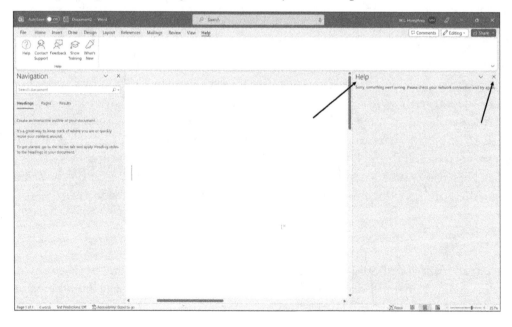

To close a task pane, click on the X in the top right corner of the pane. That arrow next to the X also allows you to move or resize the pane.

If you close a task pane and later need it, clicking on that task or using a Control shortcut for the related task will reopen it. To reopen the Navigation task pane, for example, you can use Ctrl + F, which is the control shortcut for Find.

Control Shortcuts

There are various shortcuts that you can use to perform common tasks in Word, such as Ctrl + C to copy. When I refer to those tasks, I will write them like I just did this one with the name of the keys that need to be used to execute the shortcut, separated by a plus sign. So Ctrl + C means hold down both the Ctrl key and the C key at the same time.

Even though I will write them using a capital letter, they do not require you to use a capital letter. Just hold down the letter indicated and you'll be fine. So Ctrl and the c key at the same time will copy your selection.

Absolute Basics

Now that we've established a common set of terms to use and you know how to make your screen look like mine, it's time to cover the absolute basics of opening, saving, closing, deleting, and renaming a Word file.

Open Word

If you're new to using Microsoft Word, then the first thing you need to learn is how to open it. The simplest way to open Word is to double-click on an existing Word file. That will not only open that file, but also open Word.

But if you don't have a file to open or don't want to open Word that way, then you have a few choices. The first is to go to your Start menu, which in Windows is usually located at the bottom of the screen. I always set mine so that it's in the left corner, but I believe the current Windows default puts it towards the center instead.

In Windows 11, left-click on the Windows icon and then find the Word icon in your pinned apps list or recently-used list. Here I've clicked on the Windows icon and then you can see that I have Word as one of my pinned programs:

If you can't see it there, then you can either type Word into the search bar at the top of the dropdown menu or you can click on All Apps and find it in the alphabetical listing of all of your applications.

I personally prefer to add the Word icon to my taskbar at the bottom of my screen so that I don't have to find it every time. Once it's there I can just left-click on the icon once to open Word.

You can see the Word icon in the taskbar in the screenshot above. It's the fourth one from the right at the very bottom of the screen, next to the ones for Excel, PowerPoint, and Access.

To put an icon in your taskbar, right-click on the application in the Start menu and choose Pin To Taskbar from the dropdown menu.

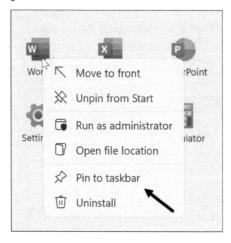

Once an icon has been added to your taskbar, you can left-click the icon and drag it to place it in the order you want. For example, I have my internet browsers grouped, then my Office programs, and then my audio/video programs.

New Word File

By default, Word is going to open to a Welcome screen.

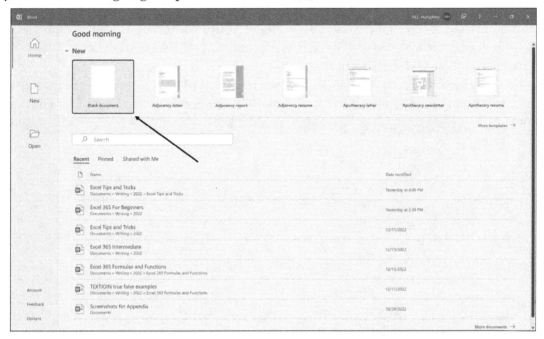

Click on Blank Document at the top to open a brand-new Word document. You can see in that same row that there are also a number of templates available to you. For this book, we're not going to use them. I think in the last ten years I've only used a Word template once.

For most basic writing tasks, you don't need them. But if you want to, feel free to explore them. You can see what each one will look like in the thumbnail and there is a More Templates option to click on at the end of that list.

You can also click on New on the left-hand side to start a new document but that will just take you to another screen that has Blank Document at the top and then a number of templates listed below that. So it's not necessary to do and doesn't give you any special options that you don't already have on the Welcome screen.

If you are already in a Word document and want to open an additional new Word document, you can use Ctrl + N to do so. Your other option is to go to the File menu up top which will take you back to the Welcome screen, and then click on Blank Document from there.

Open Existing Word File

To open an existing Word file, one option is to go to the file wherever you have it saved and double-click on it.

If it's a file I haven't used recently, this is generally the option I choose because I find it easier (or maybe more consistent) to navigate to my files outside of Word rather than through Word.

Your other option is to open Word first and then find the file you want to open through Word. This is the option I choose for files I've used recently.

On the Welcome screen there will be a listing of your Recent files as well as a tab you can click on to locate any files you've Pinned. (As you can see in the screenshot above.) If you see the file you want, just left-click on it.

The Open screen, which you can access by clicking on Open on the left-hand side or by using Ctrl + O has more options, so I want to walk through that one in detail. Here it is:

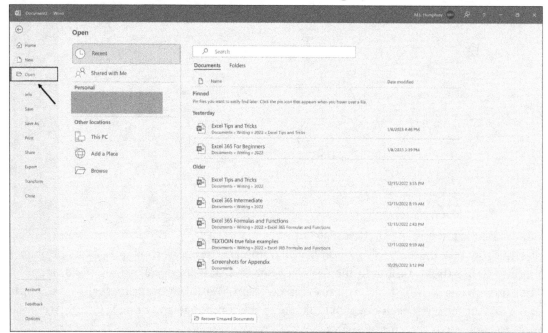

On the right-hand side is a listing of recently-used Word documents. You can see here that there are seven files listed for me right now in chronological order from most-recently-used to oldest. If you want to open one of those files, simply click on the name and the file will open.

If you have any files that you always want to have available to you, you can Pin those files and then they will be available in that Pinned section up top. (I'll show you how to do that in a moment.)

The default is a listing of your documents, but you can also click on Folders under the Search bar to see a list of folders that contain recently-opened documents:

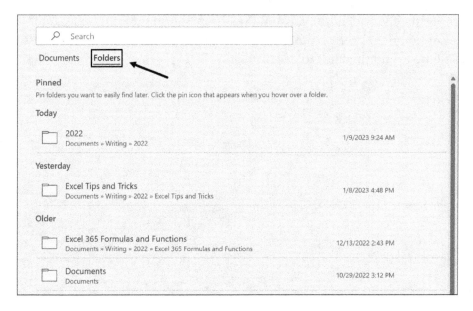

This is useful for when the file you want isn't listed, but it's located in a folder that you use often. For example, my 2022 folder has all folders and documents I worked on related to my writing in 2022.

Click on the folder name and that will show you any files in that folder as well as any sub-folders. You can keep navigating to the file you want by clicking through those sub-folders.

So, for example, here I clicked on 2022 in that original listing, and then the AML Compliance folder, and now I have four files I can choose from even though they weren't files I'd used recently:

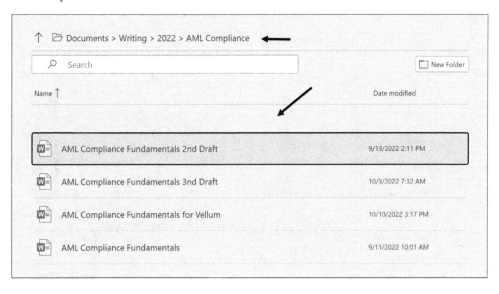

You can see the file path at the top and the list of files in the main space.

Another option if neither of those work is to navigate using the locations listed between the left-hand menu and the files/folders listing.

Right now I have the option to click on This PC, Browse, or OneDrive. (I personally don't use OneDrive because I'm a weird paranoid person and don't like storing my data "out there" somewhere, but it all works the same.)

If I click on Browse, that will open the Open dialogue box, which will then let me navigate to any file location on my computer and open my file from there:

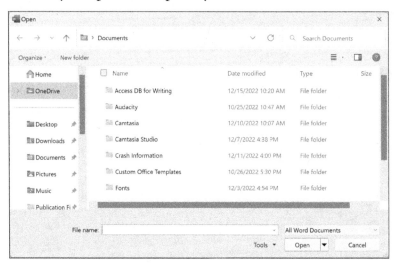

Double-click on each of the folders in the main space (like Access DB for Writing) to open them or click once on the options on the left-hand side (like Desktop) to move to a location.

Once you find your Word document, click on it and then click on Open, or double-click on it to open it.

Pin a File

To pin a file, open it so that it's in your Recent files listing and then hold your mouse over that listing in the Welcome or Open screen.

On the right-hand side of the listing, under Date Modified you should see a little thumbtack image:

When you hold your mouse over it, it will say "Pin This Item to the List". Click on the thumbtack and the file will move to the Pinned section.

In the Welcome screen, that's a separate section where you have to click on Pinned to see it:

In the Open screen where we were before, it's just listed in a special area at the top of the list.

To unpin a file, just click on the thumbtack image again.

Close a File

To close a file, you have a few options there as well. I usually click on the X in the top right corner:

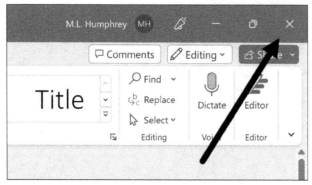

You can also go to the File tab and then choose Close from the left-hand menu. Or you can use Ctrl + W to close the current workbook.

The X in the top corner will also close out Word if you only had one file open or no files open.

Another option, if you have Word pinned to your taskbar, is to right-click on the Word icon and choose to Close Window (if you have one Word file open) or Close All Windows (if you have multiple Word files open) from there.

If you haven't made changes to your file(s) then Word will just close the file(s). But if you have, then Word will ask about saving the file.

Save a File

There are two types of saving in Word.

You can use Save to save an existing file as-is with the same name and location and file type. That will take the prior version of the file and overwrite it with the file as it exists right now.

Or you can use Save As which is for new files that don't already have a location or name as well as for existing files where you want to change the name, location, or file type or where you want to keep the old version as it was and also create a new version.

Let's walk through all of those scenarios now.

If you try to close a new file without saving first, Word will bring up a dialogue box asking if you want to save your changes to that file:

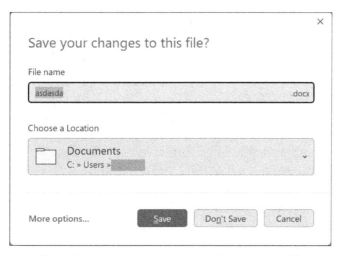

If you want to close the file without saving it, click on Don't Save. If you want to keep the file open for the time being and not save yet, click on Cancel.

If you do want to save the file, then give it a name in the File Name field, which should be highlighted by default.

Word will also display a default save location below that. In my case, it's my local Documents folder because I changed my options. Yours may default to OneDrive.

You can change the location by clicking on the dropdown arrow. That will show a list of options to choose from. For me, that list is recent locations I've saved to.

If none of those options work for you, click on More Locations at the bottom of the dropdown menu or More Options in the dialogue box. Both will open the Save As dialogue box:

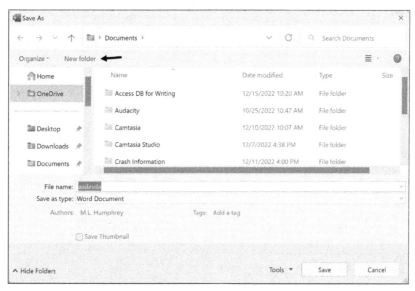

From there you can navigate to wherever you want to save your document. Note that at the top there is also an option for New Folder in case you want to save the file into a folder that doesn't already exist. Just navigate to where you want that folder to be, create it, name it, hit enter, and then select it to save to it.

Click on Save when you're ready.

Going back to the first dialogue box that appeared, you can see that Word 365 as of January 2023 defaults to using the .docx file type.

As of now, I'd say that's probably a fine format to use. Files that were created in any version of Word prior to Word 2007 were .doc files and for anyone working in one of those older versions of Word, they can't open a .docx file.

But I think at this point we're far enough away from that changeover that most people are able to open the newer file version and you're fine to always work in it.

(Five years ago, that was not my advice.)

If, however, you ever run into a situation where that isn't the case, then note that in the Save As dialogue box you can change the file type using that Save As Type dropdown:

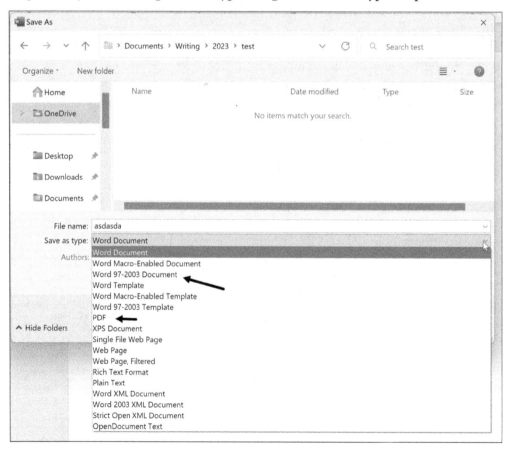

The option to use for older versions of Word is Word 97-2003 document. Also, this is where you can have Word save a document for you as a PDF file, which I've needed a few times.

(If you save as a PDF, however, be careful if the document you're using has images and image quality is important because the default image quality in Word is not a high enough standard for commercial printing. You may need to convert to a PDF using the Adobe website instead to get the quality of image you need.)

Okay. So that's one way to get to Save As. Just let Word do it for you with a new document. But if you want more control than that or if you're working with an existing document where you want to save it under a new name, new location, or new file type, then the better option is to go to File and then choose Save As on the left-hand side menu.

That will bring you to the Save As screen:

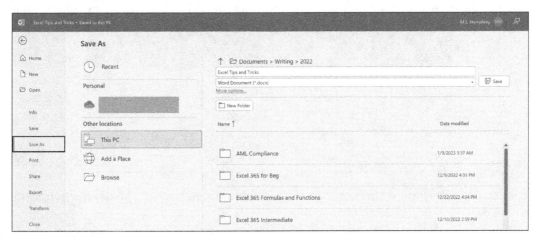

The document name and location will already be populated by default for an existing document, but you can click into the field for name to change that or you can navigate to a new location using the listed folders.

There is also a dropdown to change file format.

Once all those changes have been made, simply click on Save to save the file under its new name, location, and file type.

Clicking on More Options or Browse from this screen will open the Save As dialogue box, which we already discussed above.

I will note here that if you are just trying to move a file to a new location or trying to rename a file, this is not the way to do it, because the old version of the file will still exist. If you want to move a file or rename a file and not have that old version exist, then you need to move or rename the file outside of Word. We'll cover that in a minute.

So that was Save As. Usually, though, you'll just want to save your file before you close it.

Your first option is to just try to close the file. Word will display a dialogue box that asks if you want to save your changes. Click on Save to keep those changes, click on Don't Save to close the file without keeping the changes, or click on Cancel to keep the document open for now.

Your second option is to use Ctrl + S to save the document. You can do this at any point in time. You don't have to wait until you're ready to close the file to save your changes up to that point. I recently had a laptop that was crashing on me repeatedly, so I would use Ctrl + S after every significant change I made so that if my computer crashed I wouldn't lose that work.

(Word does have an AutoSave back-up feature. I believe the default right now is to save every 10 minutes. So you should never lose more than ten minutes of work, but when you do lose work that ten minutes can be a lot. I changed my settings to five minutes to help with that, but also saving frequently made a difference, too.)

Your third option, and again this is one you can do at any time, is to use the little disc icon at the top left corner of the screen.

It's meant to look like a little computer disc. Nobody uses those anymore, but that's what we

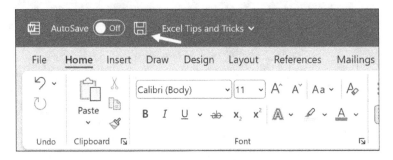

used to save information on rather than using a thumbdrive back in the day. Just click on the icon to save.

Finally, you could go to File and then choose Save, but given all the other options, that's the least efficient one to use. I just mention it because it's the most visible one.

Rename a File

As I mentioned above, if all you want to do is rename a file, doing so through Word is not the way to do it. The reason is because you end up with two files. The one with the old name and the one with the new name.

To rename a file and just have that one version of the file, you need to close the file and then go to where the file is saved. Click on the file once to select it. Click on it again to make the name editable. (The name will be highlighted when that happens.) And then make your changes and hit enter.

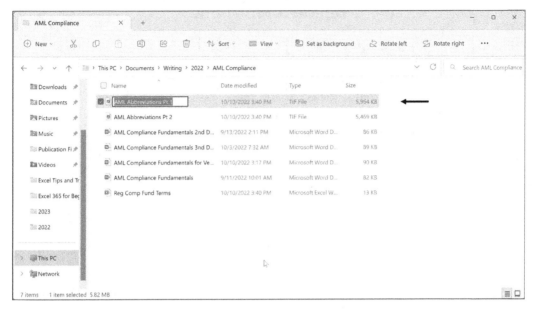

(You could also right-click on the file name, choose Show More Options, and then choose Rename from the dropdown menu, but the click and then click again option is faster and more consistent.)

When you rename a file, you cannot then open the file from your recent files listing. It may still display there under the old name, but you will get an error message that Word can't find the file. So the next time you open it you need to do so either from its current location or by navigating to the file through Word.

Move a File

As with renaming a file, the best way to relocate a file is to do so outside of Word so you don't end up with multiple copies.

Find the file where it's currently located, click on it, use Ctrl + X to cut it from its current location, go to where you want to move the file, and use Ctrl + V to paste it.

(And again, you could do this with right-click and finding the menu options for Cut and Paste, but the control shortcuts are faster.)

As with renaming a file, when you move a file you will then need to open that file directly the next time you use it in Word because the recent file listing won't work.

I often run into this issue because I have a habit of tidying up when I finish a project. I move my files into a Published sub-folder. Since that relocates the files, the next time I want to open them in Word, they're no longer where they were, so Word can't find them.

Delete a Word File

Finally, we need to discuss how to delete a Word file. Once more, this cannot be done in Word itself. You need to navigate to where the file is saved.

Click on the file name so that it's selected and then click on the trash can icon at the top of the dialogue box. Or, click on the file name and use the Delete key.

Or, you can right-click on the file name and click on the trash can icon there. Or, you can right-click on the file name, choose Show More Options, and then choose Delete from the dropdown menu.

Many available choices. The key is that it must be done where the file is saved and can't be done through Word.

Inputting Information

Now it's time to talk about how to actually input information in Word.

At its most basic, inputting information in Word is very easy to do if you're not working with a template. Simply open a new Word document and start typing.

But there are a few things in Word 365 that you may not like and so want to turn off. And there are some general tips and tricks I want to share with you to make using Word easier.

First up, Text Predictions.

Text Predictions

One of the unpleasant surprises I had when I first started using Word 365 in late 2022 was that it defaults to having Text Predictions turned On. What this does is as you type, it tries to figure out what the next words you want are and it suggests them for you. It was highly distracting for me and I immediately wanted it gone.

Of course, this morning as I was trying to demonstrate this so I could take a screenshot and show you, it let me write entire paragraphs without making any suggestions. The only example I could get to work was this one:

Why isn't Word text prediction working for me right now? Tab

I typed the words "Why isn't Word text prediction working for me right" and then typed a space.

Word suggested "now?" to complete the sentence.

You can see that in the screenshot above. The suggested text is a light gray instead of black and it shows Tab next to that text. If I wanted to use the suggestion, I could use the Tab key or the right arrow key and Word would insert the suggested text for me and then I could keep going with the next text I want to type.

For me, as someone who did not grow up with predictive text, that interferes with my writing ability. It makes me slow down and assess whether the suggestion is an accurate one or not and then I have to think to use a Tab or right arrow key to accept that change.

But if you're new to Word then it might really help speed up your writing. Especially if you're writing something where it wants to make suggestions for you.

The first time I used Word 365 if felt like it was suggesting every other word to me. Now I'm writing entire paragraphs and it isn't.

My preference is to just turn it off. If you also want to do that, then go to the bottom left side of the screen and click on Text Predictions.

That will bring up the Word Options dialogue box to the Advanced tab.

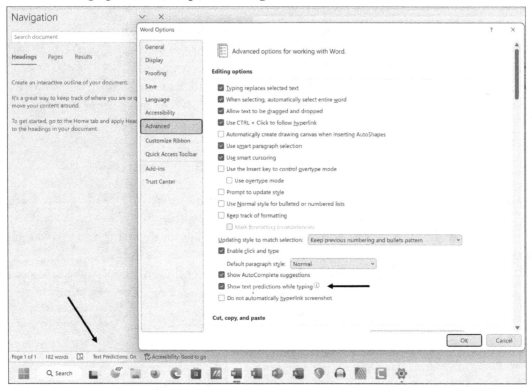

Click on the box for "Show Text Predictions While Typing" to turn that off. Once you've done that, you can just type what you want to type and Word will not have an opinion on it. Well, at least not about what the next word should be. It will still, by default, have opinions about your spelling and grammar.

So let's talk about that next.

Spelling and Grammar Flags As You Type

Here are a few of those paragraphs I typed trying to get it to make a prediction:

> I want to write something that is very basic and simple so that Word will predict what I am going to write next. It would help if Word would suggest a word for me now and again so that I can see how text prediction actually works in Word and tell others about it. But right now I'm doing a lot of typing and not seeing anything happen.
>
> What do I have to type to have Word predict my next words. There was a door in between me and my destination. Nope, that didn't work. What other phrases can I type that Word will understand in time to make a suggestion for me?
>
> I was able to get it to work on why isn't Word working for me right now? But now it won't do it again and I don't understand.

If you look closely at the text (because they've made this less obvious in the latest version of Word), you will see that some of my text has a dotted blue line under it and some of my text has a double blue underline.

You can right-click on the flagged text to see what Word's identified issue is:

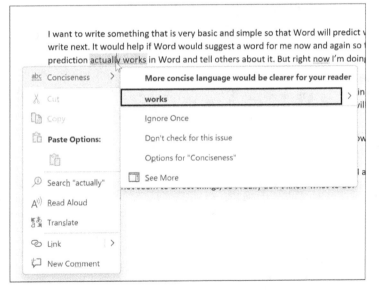

So, here, for the dotted blue line it is telling me that I could use more concise language. It would prefer that I use "prediction works in Word" instead of "prediction actually works in Word."

If I agree, I can click on that suggested text and it will change it for me.

I can also tell it to ignore that one suggestion or to stop checking for that particular issue by clicking on those options in the dropdown.

Here is one of the double-underlined examples:

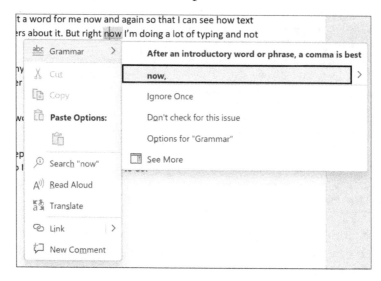

In this case, it thinks I'm violating a grammar rule. According to Word, a comma is best after an introductory word or phrase. It wants me to have used "But right now, I'm…" instead of "But right now I'm…"

Fair enough.

Personally, I don't want to stop while I'm writing and consider grammar issues, so I often will have this turned off in my version of Word.

But before I show you how to do that, let's misspell a few things. Here I've gone back to the first paragraph and deliberately misspelled "write" and "basic". For spelling errors, Word uses a red squiggly line under the text.

I want to writte something that is very basiic and simple so that Word will predict what I am going to write next. It would help if Word would suggest a word for me now and again so that I can see how text prediction actually works in Word and tell others about it. But right now I'm doing a lot of typing and not seeing anything happen.

Once more, you can right-click on the word that was flagged and Word will provide suggestions:

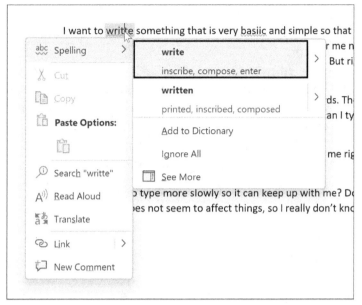

In this case, it also includes a brief definition of each suggested word so that you can choose between, for example, discrete and discreet, correctly.

If the word that it flagged is one that you use often that was not recognized by Word, you can click on the Add to Dictionary option to add that word into the dictionary that Word uses for your documents so it's not flagged anymore.

I usually do not do this, just in case I'm wrong. What I instead do is use the Ignore All option which will ignore all uses of that word in that document. But you need to know that it's very specific. It will only do that form of that word and will not include plurals or possessives.

Let me show you:

Here I have two sentences that use two made-up words, "Gramdy's favorite past time was to play with gregorns. Gramdy really like a good gregorn."

(I'm leaving that typo in there so we can discuss that in a minute.)

In that second sentence, I told Word to ignore both "Gramdy" and "gregorn". But note that "Gramdy's" and "gregorns" are still flagged as spelling errors in the first sentence.

That's because when you choose the Ignore All option, Word will only ignore that very specific combination of letters. It doesn't extrapolate to possessives or plurals.

Which is fine. You just need to know that's the case, because likely you will also end up needing to tell it to ignore a possessive or a plural as well.

Now, let's go back to that second sentence. "Gramdy really like a good gregorn." That should be liked not like. Or maybe likes if we didn't have the first sentence to give the past tense use. But like is not correct.

And yet, it was not flagged.

You can't rely 100% on the grammar and spelling check in Word. It misses things sometimes. It's also wrong sometimes. And it has a very specific approach to grammar that is not necessarily the appropriate choice for writing fiction or less-formal prose. Also, be very careful when it flags its vs it's because about 20% of the time it gets it wrong.

I personally prefer to run the spelling and grammar check at the end rather than try to deal with that as I'm typing. So let's cover two things, real quick. One, how to turn off grammar check as you're typing as well as how to turn off specific rules. And, two, how to run a spelling and grammar check on your entire document.

Turn Off Grammar or Spell Check as You Type

To disable the grammar or spelling check as you type, go to File and then choose Options at the bottom-left corner of the screen to open the Word Options dialogue box. Go to the Proofing tab.

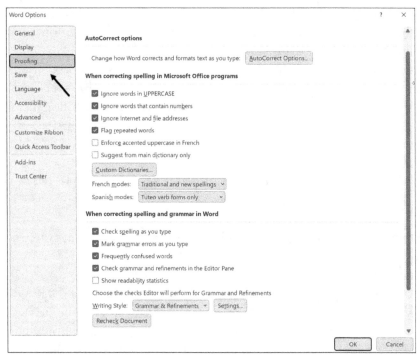

You can see that there are a number of options here. The ones that are blue and checked are the ones that are currently active.

To turn off grammar and/or spelling checks as you type, go to the section titled When Correcting Spelling and Grammar in Word and then check the box for "Check Spelling As You Type" and/or "Mark Grammar Errors As You Type" to turn them off.

My preference is to usually turn off grammar check but leave on spellcheck. That's because I'm usually catching and correcting a misspelled word as soon as I type it so I don't find that distracting in the same way I do the grammar error flags.

Run a Spelling and Grammar Check On Your Document

Where I do the bulk of my spelling and grammar check is at the end when the document is finished. I go to the Proofing section of the Review tab and click on the Spelling and Grammar option:

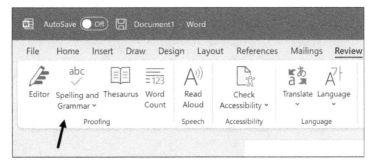

(The dropdown menu there will let you choose to just review Spelling instead if you want.)

When you click on Spelling and Grammar, an Editor task pane will open on the right-hand side of the workspace and you'll see the first identified issue:

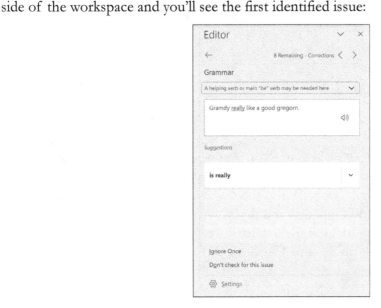

In this case it was a grammar issue. It shows the sentence that contains the error, flags the text that was identified as an issue, and then below that lists a suggestion for how to fix it.

You can either click on the suggestion to apply it, click on Ignore Once, click on the option to not check for this issue, or use the arrows at the top of the task pane to move to the next identified issue.

Here it is for a spelling error:

If you click on a solution, like I just clicked on basic for that spelling error, it will immediately move to the next flagged issue, so be careful on that one that you don't make a mistake.

Another option you have is to go directly into the document and make your change there. So, for example, maybe it flagged "Gramdy" and that is wrong, but none of the suggestions are right because it's supposed to be Gramby. In that case, you can click into the document, make your change, and then click on Resume Checking Corrections when you're done.

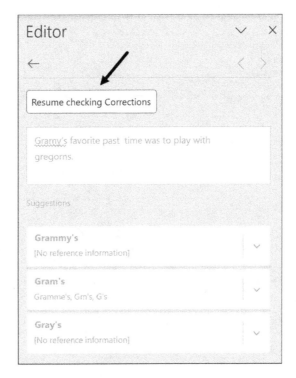

AutoCorrect

Another thing that Word likes to do to help, and sometimes it is a help, is to autocorrect common errors. One of my personal issues is that I will often type "teh" instead of "the". Word knows this happens a lot so it changes that immediately as soon as I move on to the next word.

Which is great when you want that to happen. But it's something to watch out for. For example, I had to undo that change when it did it to me above. (Ctrl + Z will do that if you notice it right away.)

It also has certain tricks that you can use to type common symbols or characters. Often those are great to have around, like the double hyphen that gets turned into a dash, but sometimes they get in the way. My background is in securities regulation. So I am far more likely to write about Rule 3070(c) than I am to need the copyright symbol. But by default in Word using (c) creates the copyright symbol.

You can turn off any AutoCorrect option you want in the Word Options dialogue box. In this case I opened the dialogue box by clicking on Text Prediction at the bottom of the workspace and then went to the Proofing page. At the top is an AutoCorrect options button that will open the AutoCorrect dialogue box when you click on it:

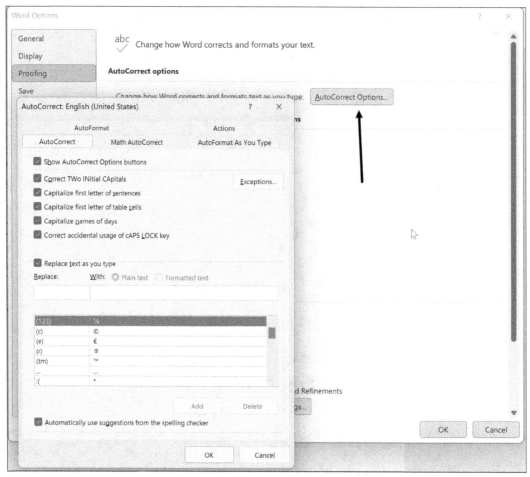

You can see both dialogue boxes in the image above.

Uncheck any option you don't want Word to use. You can also click on one of those AutoCorrect choices that's listed down below, like turning (123) into one-eighth and then click on Delete to remove it. And you can add your own custom autocorrect options if you want using the Add option.

For some options, like replacing straight quotes with smart quotes, you may need to turn it off on more than one tab. Both the AutoFormat tab and the AutoFormat As You Type tab sometimes overlap.

Undo

I just mentioned this above, but if you ever do anything in Word that you want to undo, the best way to do so is to use Ctrl + Z. That will undo the last thing you did. So if AutoCorrect changes something you didn't want it to change, Ctrl + Z will reverse that.

It can also undo formatting or typing or anything else. With text it often undoes a word or phrase at a time so may undo more than you want.

There is also an Undo menu option on the far left-hand side of the Home tab. It has a dropdown menu that lets you undo multiple steps at once.

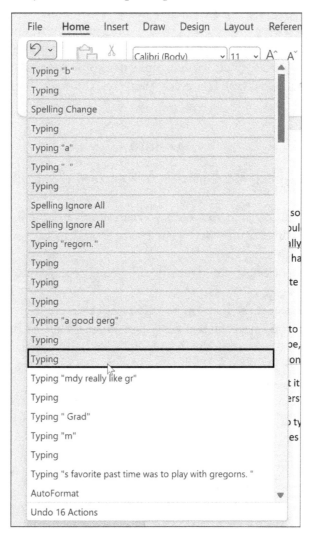

The further down that list you click, the more steps you will undo. As you move your mouse down that list you will see all of the steps above highlighted in gray to indicate that those steps will all be undone when you make that selection. In the screenshot above I'd be undoing 16 actions at once if I made that selection.

Redo

If you ever undo something and change your mind, you can Redo. Ctrl + Y will redo the last action.

There is also a Redo option on the left-hand side of the Home tab, but in Word you can only redo one action at a time so the dropdown doesn't give any additional choices.

If you have no action that you undid, Ctrl + Y or the Redo option in the Home tab will perform the last task you performed. For example, if I apply italics to text, Ctrl + Y will then let me apply italics again. Same with text color, font, etc. Although I found it to be glitchy with text highlight color.

Delete

Finally, if you type something you don't want to keep, then you need to remove that text by deleting it.

There are a few options open to you. First, you can simply use the Backspace key to remove any text one letter at a time from where your cursor is and to the left. (When you're in the document the cursor is a vertical line.)

If you are for some reason on the right side of the text you want to delete, use the Delete key instead.

Another option is to select the text you want to remove first (left-click and drag or use Shift and the arrow keys.) If you select the text first, then either Delete or Backspace will work.

You could also Cut the text using the dropdown menu in the main workspace or from the Clipboard section of the Home tab. We'll talk about Cut more in the next chapter when we talk about moving your text around.

Moving Information

Once you have information in your document, there may come a time when you need to move that information around. Maybe you want to reorder the document or maybe you wrote part of a report and someone else wrote another part in another Word document and now you want to combine those two.

Let's talk now about how to do that.

Select All

First up, if you want to select everything in a document, including text, images, and headers/footers, you can do so using Select All. The easiest way is to use Ctrl + A.

You can also go to the Editing section of the Home tab and click on Select to open the dropdown menu there which will then let you choose to Select All, Select Objects, Select All Text with Similar Formatting, or to open the Selection Pane which will list any objects (like shapes or charts) in your document.

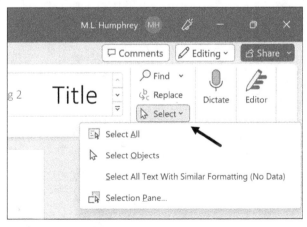

For our purposes in this book, that first option, Select All, is the one to remember.

You may also at some point want to use Select Text With Similar Formatting to easily change the formatting of different selections from your document at once. For example, when I write these books I use bolded text for the section headers within each chapter. If I decide that I want to quickly apply a different font size, font, font color, etc. to all of those headings at once, I can use this option and then apply my formatting (which we will cover soon) and all similarly-formatted entries will update.

Okay. Now let's go back to that example where you have two documents and you want to take the text from one and put it in the other. Step one was to select all of that text. For me, that's Ctrl + A. Done.

Copy or Cut Text

The next step would then be to copy or to cut that text. When you Copy, you keep the text where it was originally and take a copy of it. When you Cut, you remove the text from its original location and have a copy of it that you can paste elsewhere.

So the choice of which one to use comes down to whether you want to leave a version in the original location. In our example here where we're taking text from one document and putting it in another, it really doesn't matter. Because even if I Cut that text from the first document as long as I close that document without saving changes, that document remains as it was.

When moving sections of text around within a document, use Cut. When reusing text from one location in another, use Copy.

How to do this.

The simplest way, and definitely memorize these, is to use the Control shortcuts. Ctrl + C will copy. Ctrl + X will cut. Select your text first and then use the shortcut you want.

If you don't remember the shortcuts or don't want to use them, then you can right-click after selecting your text and choose Copy or Cut from the dropdown menu:

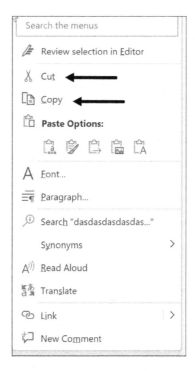

Your final option is to go to the Clipboard section of the Home tab and choose the cut or copy option from there. Cut is represented by a pair of scissors. Copy is represented by two pages stacked on top of each other. (We'll see that in a moment when we discuss how to paste text.)

Paste Text

Once you have selected your text and copied or cut that text, then it's time to paste the text. Go to the point in the document where you want to place the text and, if you have no special changes that need to be made to that text, simply use Ctrl + V to paste it.

Your other options are to right-click and choose one of the Paste options from the dropdown menu. (See above.) Or to go to the Clipboard section of the Home tab and click on the Paste option there.

If you want to paste the text but with changes, then you need to use one of the Paste Special options available either through the dropdown menu in the main workspace or by clicking on the dropdown arrow under Paste in the Clipboard section of the Home tab:

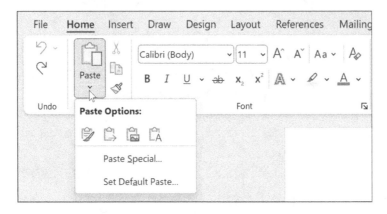

Clicking on Paste Special in that dropdown will bring up the Paste Special dialogue box, but we're just going to cover the four options you can see there which are, from left to right, Keep Source Formatting, Merge Formatting, Picture, and Keep Text Only.

For basic text that doesn't have a lot of formatting and where the source and destination formatting is similar, you won't see much difference between those options. But often I find I need this when someone, for example, wrote their portion of a document in the default Word font (Calibri) and now I'm pasting that into a document using a different font like Times New Roman. Or when I'm taking text from Excel and need to paste it into a formatted Word document.

Let's look at a very basic example:

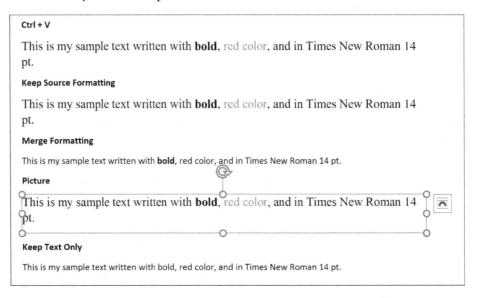

I took a sentence and I changed the font to Times New Roman, 14 point (so larger), changed the text "red color" to red, and applied bold formatting to the word "bold". I then selected that text and pasted it into a new Word document which by default is using Calibri 11 point font.

That first example is using Ctrl + V and the text pasted in exactly like it was formatted in the first document. Same for the next option where I used Keep Source Formatting.

Where things get interesting is starting with the Merge Formatting option. It kept the bolded text, but changed the font, font size, and font color.

Picture looks like it's the same as the first two options, but you can see that I clicked on that one to show you that it's in fact a picture now. You cannot edit or format that text, it's like taking a snapshot of the text and dropping it into the document.

Finally, Keep Text Only pasted the text in but removed the bolding and red text and also changed the font and font size to the default for the document the text was pasted into.

Usually, when I need one of these options, it is the Keep Text Only option I need so that whatever I'm pasting into the document matches what's already there.

One final thing to note. It is possible to have multiple snippets of text copied or cut at one time and to then be able to paste all or one of them into your document. To see which text snippets are available to you to paste, you need to open the Clipboard task pane.

To do that, click on the expansion arrow in the Clipboard section of the Home tab. You should see something like this on the left-hand side of your workspace:

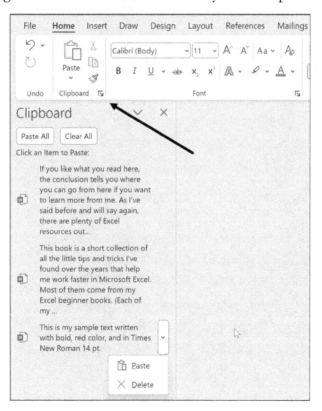

You can click on an individual entry to paste it. Or you can click on the arrow next to the snippet like I have above and choose Paste that way. Or you can use that Paste All option at the top to paste all of the snippets at once.

If you don't want one of those snippets there, click on the arrow next to it and choose Delete. (The arrow only shows when you hold your mouse over each snippet.)

I will admit I've never used this in real-life. But it's there if you need it. And could be very useful if you have multiple phrases or sections of text that you will need to paste into a document multiple times. You could copy each of them and then just quickly go through and click on the one you need to paste it into the document as it's needed.

* * *

Okay, so that was the easy part of working in Word. Open a new document and type away and then copy or cut and paste your text around as needed. Now we get into the "fun" of formatting, starting with text formatting, some of which you've seen me do already.

Text Formatting

Text and paragraph formatting is key to working in Word. I have yet to work for an employer who wanted their staff to use Calibri as the font on documents. And I don't think I've ever written a book that didn't use italics or bold. So this chapter is a very important one to master if you're going to use Word.

The text formatting options can be accessed in a number of ways.

First, there are control shortcuts for some of the most basic formatting like Bold (Ctrl + B), Italics (Ctrl + I), and Underline (Ctrl + U).

Second, in the Font section of the Home tab you can find the most common formatting choices:

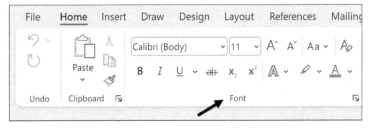

Third, the expansion arrow there as well as right-clicking and choosing Font from the dropdown menu in your document will both open the Font dialogue box. This can also be opened by using Ctrl + D.

Finally, there is a mini formatting menu that you can see if you right-click in your document:

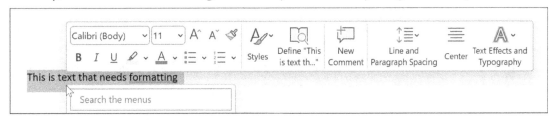

For each of the above options, first select the text you want to format, and then apply the formatting option using the method you prefer.

Let's now walk through what your formatting options are. I'm going to do this alphabetically so you can easily return to this chapter when needed, although you can also use the index in the back of the print version of this book or search in the ebook.

Bold

To bold text I usually just use Ctrl + B.

The Font dialogue box allows you to choose either Bold or Bold Italic.

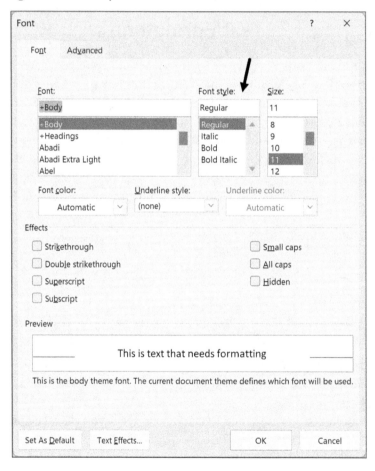

You can also click on the capital B on the left-hand side of the Font section of the Home tab or the mini formatting menu.

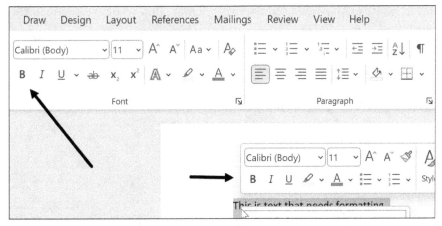

To remove bolding from text, you can either use Ctrl + B again, click on the capital B once more, or in the Font dialogue box change the Font Style to Regular or Italic.

For the first three options, if the text you selected was partially bolded and partially not, the first time you select the option it will bold all of the text, so you will need to do it twice to remove the bolding. (That usually happens to me if I select a range of text and there's a space at the end that wasn't formatted as bold that I can't tell isn't formatted the same way.)

Change Case

It is possible to change your selected text so that all of the letters are in uppercase, lowercase, sentence case (where the first letter of each sentence is upper case but the rest is lower case), toggle case (where the first letter of each word is lower case and the rest are in upper case), or where each word is capitalized but the rest of the letters are lower case.

I do this through the Font section of the Home tab using the Change Case option in the top row on the right-hand side. It's represented by an Aa where there is a capital letter A next to a lower-case one.

Here you can see the dropdown choices as well as examples of each one in the document:

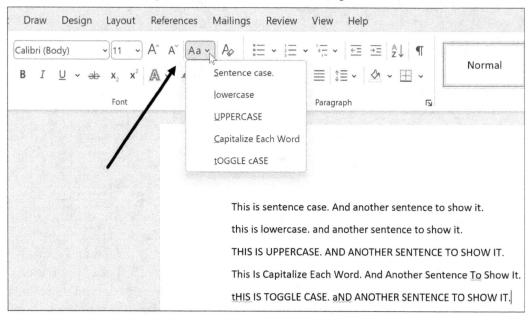

Change case is also an option in the mini formatting menu.

The Font dialogue box also has checkboxes for Small Caps and All Caps.

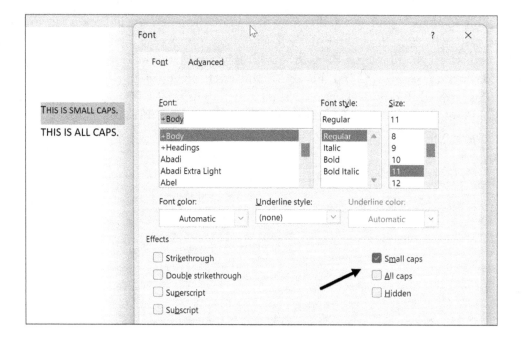

Font Color

Font color is another one that I usually apply using the Font section of the Home tab. It's the A with a red line under it, at least by default. (Once you change the color that new color will be the color under the A.) It is also available in the mini formatting menu as well as in the Font Color dropdown menu of the Font dialogue box.

In the Home tab, if you just want the color shown under the A (which is red by default), click on the A. Otherwise, click on the dropdown arrow to see seventy different font colors you can choose from:

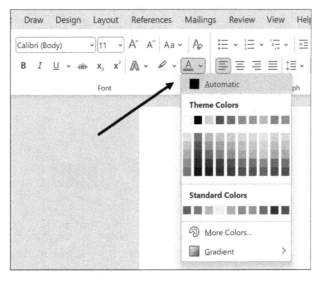

If one of those seventy colors isn't what you want or you have a specific color that you're required to use, click on More Colors to bring up the Colors dialogue box.

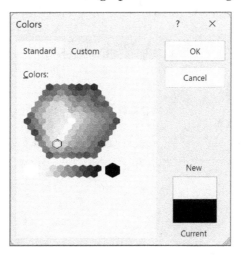

The first tab of that dialogue box is labeled Standard and shows a honeycomb of colors. Click on any of those colors in the honeycomb or in the white-to-gray-to-black line below that to choose a color. The new color will show at the top of the square in the bottom right corner of the dialogue box. The old color will show on the bottom of that square.

Click OK to apply the new color or use the X in the top right corner to close the dialogue box without applying a new color.

If you need to use a custom color, click over to the Custom tab.

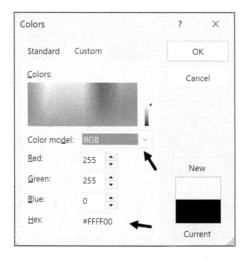

It has a rainbow color grid that you can click into and then use the slider on the side to adjust the degree of black included in the color. But the real power in this tab is below that. The dropdown lets you choose between RGB or HSL colors and there is also a Hex Code box at the very bottom.

If you have a custom color you must use, which many corporations do, you can get the exact color you need by providing the RGB, HSL, or Hex Code value on this tab. Once you've done so, click OK to apply it to your selected text.

The mini formatting menu and Font dialogue box work the exact same way. They both have a dropdown menu of colors to choose from.

Font Size

If you ever need to change the size of your text, there are a number of options available. The one I use is the dropdown menu in the top row of the Font section of the Home tab:

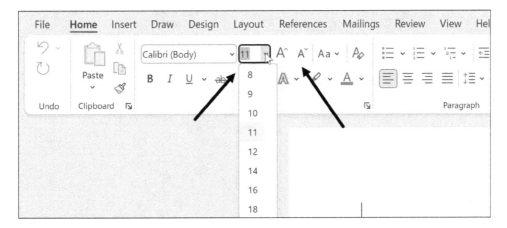

Click on the dropdown arrow and choose the font size you want from there. The default in Word is 11 pt, so a number less than that will be smaller text and a number greater than that will be larger. If you're not sure what size you want, you can hold your mouse over the different values and the text will change size within your document. To keep that change, click on the value.

You can also click into that box and type a value if you want. As you can see in the dropdown, it only includes the most popular sizes, so if you want something like 13 pt text you need to manually enter that value.

Another option is located to the right of that dropdown. There are two A's there, one with an up arrow, one with a down arrow. Clicking on those options will move the font size up or down one size. The font sizes used for that are the same as the ones in the dropdown. So you would move from 12 pt to 14 pt to 16 pt, for example.

The mini formatting menu also has those same options available. And the Font dialogue box has a list of popular font sizes to choose from as well as a box where you can type in a value.

Font Type

To the left of the font size dropdown is the Font dropdown. This is available in the Font section of the Home tab, in the mini formatting menu, and also in the Font dialogue box.

Here is the font dropdown from the Home tab:

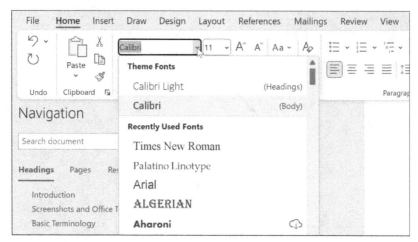

The default font in Word is Calibri. If you use a different Theme in Word you may have a different default. Those Theme Fonts will be listed first. Next you will see Recently Used Fonts listed. And then finally you will see an alphabetical listing of all available fonts.

Which fonts are listed will depend on your computer. Word comes with a number of default fonts, but it is possible to buy additional fonts as well. I have a number of those so my font listing may be different from yours.

If you know the font you want, you can click into the box with the current font name in it and start typing the font name like I've done here:

I typed "Gara" and Word took me to that portion of my fonts list and also suggested the

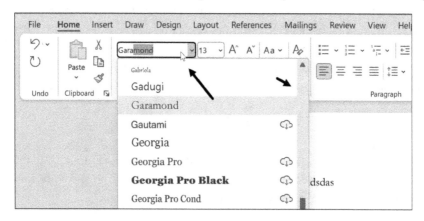

Garamond font which is the only one that starts with those letters.

There are also scroll bars available on the right-hand side of the font listing that you can use to scroll through your listed fonts.

Each font is written using that font so you can see what it looks like. That's why, for example, Georgia Pro Black is so dark compared to the rest, because a black-weight font is a very bold weight. You can also see there the difference between Gautami, which is a non-serif font, and Georgia, which is a serifed font.

Usually, in a corporate or school environment you will be told which font or fonts to use. For example, with writing, Times New Roman is a common one to use. In the past Courier was a common one. One employer I worked for preferred Palatino for everything.

If no one gives you guidance on which font to use, keep in mind your goal or purpose. In general, that is going to be legibility. You want people to be able to read the words you write.

For a standard audience reading a book like this one, that means using a serifed font, like Times New Roman or Palatino. Serifed fonts have little feet at the bottom of the letters which are supposed to make it easier to read words.

For those who have difficulty with sight, so large-print readers for example, often a non-serifed font is a better choice. For my large print fiction titles, for example, I use Verdana.

Save the display fonts (like Algerian) and script fonts (like Cochocib) for signage or book covers or report covers. And even then, be careful to make sure that people can actually read the text.

Now, there is a new quirk in Word 365 that we should also discuss and that's those little cloud download options in that font listing. Those are fonts that are available to you to use through Word, but that are not installed on your computer. To use one of those fonts, you'd need to click on that cloud to download the font.

It is possible to disable this if they annoy you and you don't want them. To do so, go to File and then click on Account at the bottom left corner of the screen. From the Account page click on Manage Settings under Account Privacy. That will open a Privacy Settings dialogue box. You can then uncheck the box for Experiences That Download Online Content.

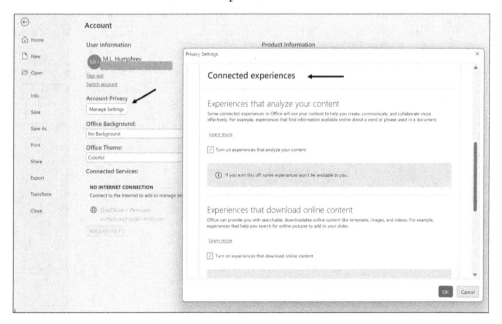

When you restart Word, you should no longer have those downloadable fonts listed. Much cleaner:

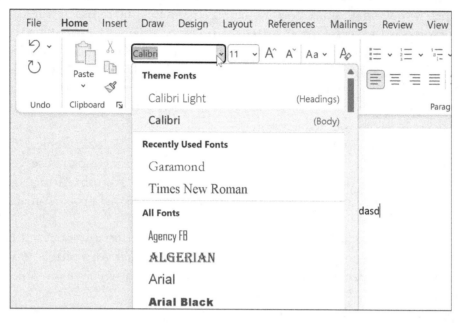

(And I should note here that I actually scrolled a little below that and unchecked the box for everything. But now I have to go and check it again so I can keep writing this book for you. There are quirks in Word 365 that are driven by those settings or by being online. For example, I learned that the Read Aloud voice in Word 365 is the old mechanical male-sounding horrible one if you're offline but a woman who almost sounds decent if you're online. Technology. Always changing.)

One more thing to mention here is that different fonts, even ones that are the same font size, will appear different sizes on the page. So choose your font before you do any final formatting or arrangement of elements.

Here are a few examples of good, solid, reliable fonts you can use that also demonstrates that:

Each of the fonts in the list above are the same font pt size.

Highlight Text

If you ever want to highlight text, like you would physically with a highlighter, you can do that using the Text Highlight Color option. By default it's going to have a bright yellow line under what looks like a marker. It's located in the bottom row of the Font section of the Home tab next to font color.

Select your text and then if all you want is yellow highlight, click on that image.

If you want to choose a different color, like I did here with a bright green, use the dropdown arrow:

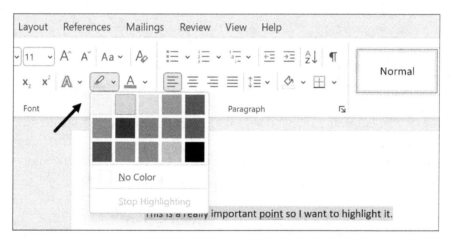

To remove a highlight, use the No Color option.

The highlight color option is also available in the mini formatting menu.

Do not confuse this with adding fill color to a cell in a table. Also, it's better to use track changes and comments to flag any issues in a document rather than use the highlighter for that purpose. Track changes, comments, and tables are intermediate-level topics covered in the next book in this series, but I just wanted to mention it here in case.

Italicize

To italicize text, the easiest way is to use Ctrl + I. But the Font section of the Home tab and the mini formatting menu also have a slanted I that you can click on in the bottom row under the font dropdown. And the Font dialogue box has options for both Italic and Bold Italic under font style.

To remove italics, select your text and then once more use Ctrl + I or click on the slanted I in the Font section of the Home tab or in the mini formatting menu. You can also change the font style back to Regular or to Bold in the Font dialogue box. As with bolding, if you select text that is partially italicized you will need to use Ctrl + I or click on the slanted I twice because the first time will apply it to all of the text and the second will remove it.

Strikethrough

To add a basic strikethrough to text, you can use the ab with a strikethrough in the Font section of the Home tab or the mini formatting menu. In the mini formatting menu it's off to the right side:

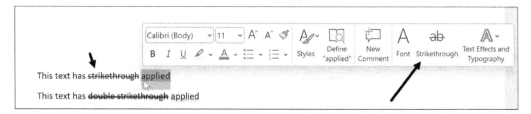

Above you can see an example of what that looks like when applied to the word "strikethrough" in the first line of text.

If you want a double strikethrough, like in the second line of text, then you need to use the Font dialogue box. There is a checkbox there for double strikethrough.

Subscript or Superscript

To apply subscript or superscript to text, use the options in the Font section of the Home tab.

Subscript looks like an X with a 2 in the subscript position. Superscript looks like an X with a 2 in the superscript position.

You can see examples of text using them in the screenshot on the next page.

Simply select the text that needs that formatting and then click on the option. So in the examples shown below, I selected the 2 in each line of text and then applied the appropriate formatting to it.

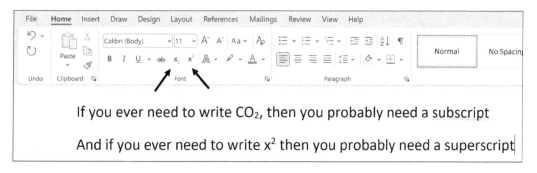

Subscript and superscript are also available as checkboxes in the Font dialogue box.

Text Effects

I'm only mentioning text effects here because they're included in the Font section of the Home tab. For new users to Word you are very unlikely to need these. But what they do is let you add an outline, shadow, reflection, glow, or other effect to your text. If you click on the dropdown arrow for Text Effects you'll see a number of pre-formatted options as well.

All I'll say here about these is that you should keep in mind your audience and effectively using text to convey your message. It is far too easy to add outlines and shadows and glow and reflections to text and end up overwhelming the text itself. So proceed with caution.

Underline

The easiest way to underline text is to use Ctrl + U. That will add a single-line underline below your selected text. You can also click on the underlined U in the Font section of the Home tab or in the mini formatting menu.

Unlike bold and italics, there is more than one underline option you can apply. To see a short list of choices, click on the dropdown arrow next to the underlined U in the Font section of the Home tab to see a list of your available choices:

There is a single line, double line, thick line, dotted line, dashed line, two lines that have both dots and dashes, as well as a wavy line.

As you hold your mouse over each option, Word will apply it to your text so you can see what it will look like. Click on the one you want.

You can also choose a color for your underline at the bottom of that dropdown.

Clicking on More Underlines will open the Font dialogue box which has an Underline Style dropdown menu with even more choices available. Select the underline style you want there and then click OK to apply it.

The Words Only option will place a single underline under each of the selected words, but not carry through that underline between the words. Like so:

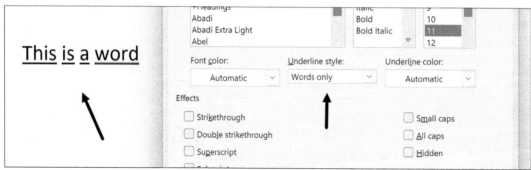

To remove an underline, use Ctrl + U or click on the underlined U once more. If you used an underline other than the default single-line option, you will have to do so twice because the first time will convert the existing underline to a single-line underline.

Another option for removing an underline is to use the dropdown for underline in the Font section of the Home tab and click on the None option towards the bottom.

The Font dialogue box also has a (none) option you can select.

* * *

Clear All Formatting

We just covered all of the formatting options in the Font section of the Home tab, but there's one more option in the top right corner there:

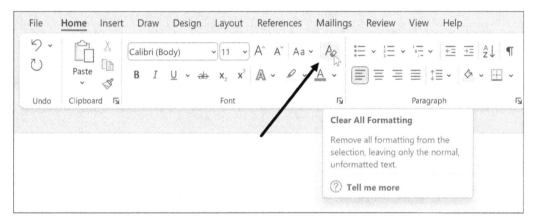

This is the Clear All Formatting option. Click on that to remove all formatting from your selected text. Below you can see text in the first row that has a change in font and font size as well as bold, italics, underline, strikethrough, text effects, highlight, and a red color applied.

> **This** is a sentence *that* I want to test
>
> This is a sentence that I want to test

In the second row is that same text after I used Clear All Formatting. It changed the font and font size back to the default of Calibri 11 pt and removed all other formatting except for the highlight.

Format Painter

The Format Painter is possibly my favorite tool in Microsoft Word. I cannot tell you how many projects I have worked on where there has been some weird slight difference between paragraphs written by different team members. No one ever knows how the change got in there and no one can figure out how to fix it.

The answer is to use the Format Painter tool. It is located in the Clipboard section of the Home tab and also available in the mini formatting menu:

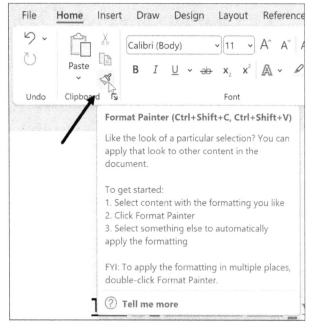

I always think of it as the format sweeper because it looks like a broom to me, but it's official name is the Format Painter.

What it does is takes the formatting of your selected text and places that formatting on other text that you select.

So step one is to select the text that has the formatting you want.

Step two is to click on the Format Painter. Double-click if you have more than one location where you want to transfer the formatting.

Step three is to select the text where you want to apply your formatting. Use the mouse or the trackpad to select the text. (Using the Shift and arrow keys doesn't work.)

If you have text that you select that has a wide variety of formatting, like in our example above for clear formatting, Word will generally go with the formatting that is at the beginning of the selection. So in that case it would transfer the bold and underline from "this" but not all the rest of the formatting.

Where Format Painter really shines in my opinion is when it's used to transfer paragraph formatting which can include the space before and after the paragraph, the space between lines in the paragraph, any indent that paragraph may have, etc. It will capture all of that.

And I don't know if this is still the case, but it's something to be aware of. Sometimes in the past it would matter whether I selected a paragraph from the first word to the last instead of from the last word to the first. So if I transferred formatting using the Format Painter and it didn't seem to fix the issue the first time, I'd go back and select the paragraph starting at the opposite end and try it again.

This can be especially true with numbered or bulleted lists.

Another trick to try is to select more than one paragraph if spacing between paragraphs matters.

Also, formatting can be transferred from one document to another. It doesn't have to be done within the same document.

When you transfer formatting this way, all of the existing formatting in the paragraph you're transferring to will be removed. It's all or nothing. (That includes italics, for example, so if you have italics in text in your document and you use the Format Painter you will lose that word-level formatting.)

If you double-click on the Format Painter so you can use it in more than one location, use Esc or click on it once more in the menu bar to turn it off when you're done.

* * *

Okay, now on to paragraph-level formatting.

Paragraph Formatting

In the last chapter the focus was on how to format individual words. Sure, you can apply that kind of formatting to every word in a document, but the formatting itself happens at the word level. Now it's time to move up to the paragraph level.

Most paragraph formatting options are located in the Paragraph section of the Home tab. Some of the options are also available in the mini formatting menu.

There is also a Paragraph dialogue box that includes the most options which can either be opened by clicking on the expansion arrow in the Paragraph section of the Home tab or by right-clicking in the main workspace and choosing Paragraph from the dropdown menu.

We are not going to cover every single option in the Paragraph section of the Home tab in this book. Multilevel lists, shading, and borders are covered in the next book in the series. As is Sort.

So, without further ado:

Paragraph Alignment

In the bottom row of the Paragraph section of the Home tab there are a series of images that show four lines. If you look closely at those lines you'll see that they represent different alignments. The left-hand one has all lines aligned along the left side, the next one has all lines centered, etc.

These are your alignment choices.

They each also have a control shortcut, which you'll see listed if you hold your mouse over each option. Align Left is Ctrl + L, Center is Ctrl + E, Align Right is Ctrl + R, and Justify is Ctrl + J.

Here are examples of all four:

> This is a sample paragraph to show you paragraph alignment. The text in this paragraph is **left-aligned**. I am going to write another sentence here just so we can get to three lines of text. Okay. Done.
>
> This is a sample paragraph to show you paragraph alignment. The text in this paragraph is **centered**. I am going to write another sentence here just so we can get to three lines of text. Okay. Done.
>
> This is a sample paragraph to show you paragraph alignment. The text in this paragraph is **right-aligned**. I am going to write another sentence here just so we can get to three lines of text. Okay. Done.
>
> This is a sample paragraph to show you paragraph alignment. The text in this paragraph is **justified**. I am going to write another sentence here just so we can get to three lines of text. Okay. Done.

Notice that with left- and right-aligned every row lines up along that side but that the opposite side is "ragged" so ends at different points. With centered each row is ragged at both ends and by an equal amount so that the line is centered within that space. With justified the spacing between the words is stretched out so that each row except the last one is lined up on both the left-hand and right-hand side.

Most documents will use either left-aligned or justified paragraphs but centered is often used for things like section headers. Right-aligned I would say is rarely used, at least in languages that read left-to-right, but it can be useful for a side note in a formatted report.

The mini formatting bar is dynamic in Word 365, meaning the choices you see will change on you. By default, I believe your paragraph options will look like this:

You can see that there is an option for Center, but not the other alignment options.

However, after I was working on this section for a bit, mine looked like this:

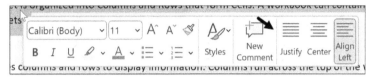

Now I can also see options for Justify and Align Left but the Line and Paragraph Spacing option is gone. At other points I've seen it with options for Center and Justify but not Align Left.

Which to me makes it an option that would not be my first choice. It's there. You can try using it. But the options in the Paragraph section of the Home tab are more consistently available.

Your final paragraph alignment formatting option is the Paragraph dialogue box which you can open by clicking on the expansion arrow in the corner of the Paragraph section of the Home tab. Alignment is available in the top section in a dropdown under General in the Indents and Spacing tab:

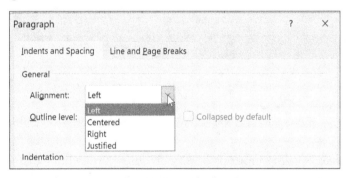

Line Spacing

Throughout school and also with submitting short stories I've always been asked to turn in double-spaced papers. But in the work world double-spaced looks horrible for a final report or memo. So chances are at some point in your life you will need to create a document that uses a different spacing than Word's default, which currently appears to be 1.08.

Here are examples of two paragraphs. The first has the default line spacing of 1.08. The second is double-spaced:

> This is a random paragraph written in Word to show you different paragraph spacing. This is the default spacing which is 1.08.
>
> This is a random paragraph written in Word to show you different paragraph spacing. This is double-
>
> spaced.

The way I usually adjust paragraph spacing is to use the Paragraph section of the Home tab. Just to the right of the alignment options in the bottom row is a dropdown menu of choices described as Line and Paragraph Spacing:

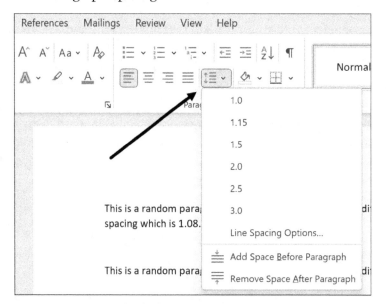

You can hold your mouse over each choice in the list to see what it will look like. Click on a choice to apply it.

If you click on Line Spacing Options in that dropdown it will open the Paragraph dialogue box. Line Spacing is located in the Spacing section on the right-hand side. There is a dropdown menu for Line Spacing there:

Sometimes I need to use that Exactly option which will then display a font size in the At box that you can adjust.

The mini formatting menu will usually also have the Line and Paragraph Spacing option which uses that same dropdown as in the Paragraph section of the Home tab, but as we saw above, not always.

There are also control shortcuts for paragraph spacing. I personally have never used them because I generally am only using one paragraph format in a document so can just use Ctrl + A to select all and then choose my format from that dropdown menu.

But if you want to use control shortcuts, Ctrl + 1 will give you single-spacing and Ctrl + 2 will give you double-spacing.

Space Between Paragraphs

I mentioned above that sometimes when formatting reports that combined portions written by different team members we'd run across a situation where the sections just didn't quite look the same. Tracking down that difference was a challenge so I'd use the Format Painter to sweep formatting from one paragraph to another. Often what was driving this was a difference in the spacing that was used between paragraphs in those different sections.

Also, this is a very useful setting to use for section headers or chapter headers. The inclination most people have is to use Enter to create space between a header and the text of that section, but the problem is that it doesn't work well when text breaks across a page. You suddenly end up with two blank lines at the top of a page, for example. Using spacing between paragraphs instead is a way to get that distance but not end up with those weird awkward blank lines in your document.

Space between paragraphs is also basically a necessity in the default way that Word formats paragraphs since there are no indents and having that space between your paragraphs is the only way to see that break in your text from paragraph to paragraph.

While the dropdown we just looked at for Line and Paragraph Spacing does have options for adding a space before a paragraph or removing a space after a paragraph, my default is to go straight to the Paragraph dialogue box for this one.

The settings are in the Spacing section on the left-hand side:

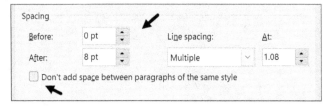

For a chapter header I put a space after. For a section header, though, I will often have values for both before and after. Same for any sort of separator. For me this is a visual setting where you basically play around with the values to see what works well for you.

You can also choose to not include those spaces when dealing with paragraphs of the same style by checking that box there.

Also, if you ever have different spacing at the bottom of one paragraph and at the top of the next, Word will use the larger of the two values, not combine them.

Keep Together

Since we're here and I'm thinking about it, I also want to mention that if you click over to the Line and Page Breaks tab in the Paragraph dialogue box that there are two useful checkboxes there.

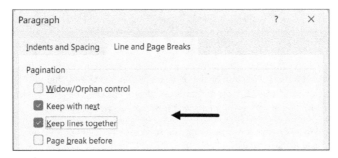

Keep With Next is good for any headers you have in your document because it will make sure that the header stays with the first paragraph of that section. Otherwise you can have a situation where your header is at the bottom of the page and then the text it's actually related to is on the next page, which doesn't look great.

Keep Lines Together is useful for if you have any headers that go across more than one line or if you ever want to make sure that all of the lines in a paragraph are displayed on the same page.

Just know that in order to make these both happen, Word is going to take all of the lines to the next page, which can result in excess white space at the bottom of the previous page. (If you're reading this book in print, you have very likely seen a few examples of that by now. I haven't formatted this book yet, but it happens in every one of these books that there is white space at the bottom of the page either to fit an image or to keep a header and its text together.)

Use these settings, though, to get that effect rather than trying to manually format your report. Because all it takes is someone adding a paragraph earlier in the document to ruin all of that manual formatting and cause you a lot of extra work.

Indents

There are two types of indents to consider. The first is the first-line indent that you see in many books that distinguishes the start of each paragraph. The second is when an entire section or paragraph is indented from the rest of the text.

The indent available in the Paragraph section of the Home tab is the full-section indent. You can click on a paragraph or select a series of paragraphs or bulleted or numbered entries (which we'll discuss in a moment) and then click on the increase indent option and it will move that text in one tab space.

Here I've taken three paragraphs and indented the second one once and the third one twice to show you what that looks like:

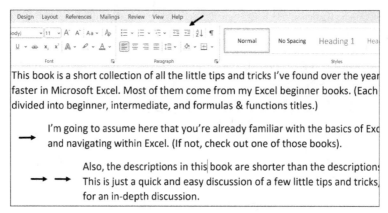

(Ignore the text, I was using a book on Microsoft Excel for the text for this one.)

To reverse an indent, use the indent option with the left-pointing arrow in the Paragraph section of the Home tab.

Once I indented those paragraphs the increase and decrease indent options were then also available on the mini formatting menu.

You can also adjust the indent using the Indentation section of the Paragraph dialogue box. See on the left-hand side in the screenshot below where the Left indent is 1". This is also where you need to go to apply a first-line indent to a paragraph.

For the first-line indent, go to the Special option in the Indentation section and click on the dropdown. Select First Line and then type a value into the By field. It's going to default to a .5" indent, but that's generally going to be too much of an indent. Here is a .2" indent where I've also removed the spacing between those two paragraphs:

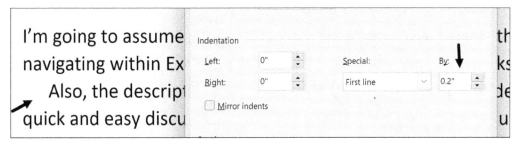

In general, you should either have spacing between your paragraphs and no first-line indent or no spacing between paragraphs but use a first-line indent. Don't do both.

Finally, another indenting option is the Tab key (and then Shift + Tab to reverse that), which will indent a single line and will create that first-line indent for you if used on a paragraph. But don't use it. There's more control and consistency in using the Paragraph dialogue box and choosing exactly the type and size of indent you want.

Bulleted Lists

Chances are that if you write enough corporate reports, at some point in time you will be asked to either create a bulleted list or a numbered list, so we're going to cover those now.

A bulleted list takes a series of text entries on different rows and puts bullet points in front of them. Like this:

- This is my first point
- This is my second one
- This is my third one and it's a real doozy.
- This is my fourth point.

Note that it indents those entries by default.

To apply bullets to a list, select your text and then go to the top row of the Paragraph section of the Home tab and click on the Bullets image. That will apply a standard bulleted list like you see above.

If you instead click on the dropdown arrow there, you can choose the type of bullet to use:

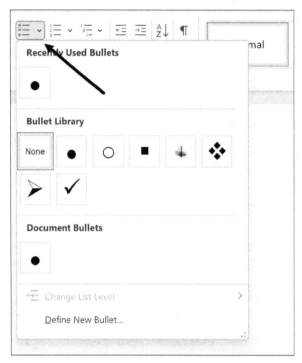

Because I just applied a bulleted list, I have a section at the top called Recently Used Bullets that shows the type of bullet I just used. Below that is the full list of bullets that you can choose from by default under the heading Bullet Library. And below that is a listing of any bullet types used in this particular document.

You can also click on that Define New Bullet option at the bottom to create a brand-new bullet type, but we're not going to do that here.

It's pretty basic to create a bulleted list.

Once a line of text is bulleted, when you hit enter from that line, the next line will also be bulleted.

You can remove that bullet by using the Backspace key, but you will still be indented to align with the text entry in the line above. If you Backspace two more times that should take you to the left-hand side of the page.

Another option is to hit Enter twice from a bulleted line. That will also remove the bullet point and take you back to the left-hand side of the page.

With bulleted lists the continuity of the list isn't an issue the way it is with numbered lists. But if you start adjusting the indent of various lines and are using bullets in multiple locations in your document you can end up with a situation where the appearance of a bulleted list on one page does not match that on another. So be careful if you go down that road.

Also, if you start a bulleted list and then have indented bullets, those indented bullets will be different by default. Like so:

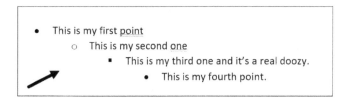

Word does this automatically as you indent each level and will automatically apply that bullet consistently for that indent level. Note that it cycled back to the first bullet type when I reached the fourth level.

You can customize this, too, using the Bullets dropdown, but exercise caution when doing so.

I indented each line there using the Tab key after clicking in front of the first letter of each row, but you can also go back to the Bullets dropdown and use the Change List Level secondary menu to choose an indent level for each line.

Shift + Tab will reverse the text one indent level.

You can also use the Decrease and Increase Indent options in the Paragraph section of the Home tab. The advantage of using those is that you can click anywhere on that line of text, you don't have to click at the start of the line like you do when using Tab or Shift + Tab.

To remove bullets from a bulleted list, select your list and then click on the bulleted list option again.

The mini formatting menu also includes the Bullets dropdown menu.

Numbered Lists

At their most basic, numbered lists work much the same way as bulleted lists. Select your rows of text and then click on the Numbering option in the top row of the Paragraph section of the Home tab. Word will turn your entries into a numbered list that looks like this:

1. This is my first point
2. This is my second one
3. This is my third one and it's a real doozy.
4. This is my fourth point.

Note that the numbered list is indented by default.

You can also start a numbered list by simply typing the first entry (1., A., etc.) and Word will convert that into a numbered list for you. (If you don't want that, just use Undo, Ctrl + X, right away.)

If you hit enter from a line that's a numbered entry it will either continue the numbering (if at the bottom of the list) or insert a new numbered entry and then renumber all other entries in the list (if in the midst of a numbered list).

You can remove a numbered entry using the Backspace key. When you do that, like I have below with what would have been number 2 in this list, Word will renumber any subsequent numbered entries to maintain a numbered list that goes from 1 to 2 to 3, etc.

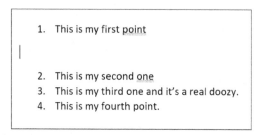

There is a Numbering dropdown menu that lets you choose other numbering styles:

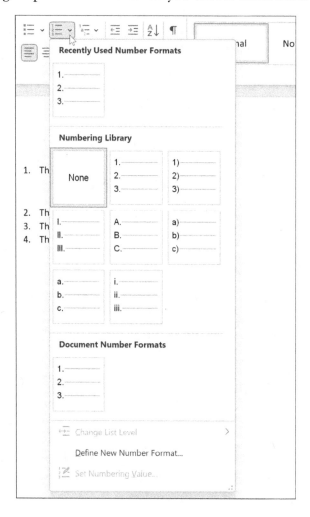

If you click on one of your numbered entries and then choose a different format from that dropdown it will change all of your entries to the new format.

Select the Set Numbering Value option at the bottom of that dropdown menu to open the Set Numbering dialogue box:

This dialogue box allows you to start a new numbered list instead of continuing the prior one or to continue a numbered list from earlier in the document. You can also choose the value for that entry.

To create a multi-level list using the Numbering option, use Tab or the Indent option to move the text to that next level. Word will automatically assign a numbering option for that next level.

Here you can see it went 1, a, i, and then back to 1 again.

> 1. This is my first item.
>   a. And here's my subpoint
>   b. And another one
>   i. And then a sub-subpoint
>   ii. And another one
>   1. And then another

When I changed the first level to an A. instead, it still went with a, i, and then 1 for the next three levels. So it doesn't follow the standard format for an outline that I was taught in school.

If you really need to go down that route, the Multilevel List option will give you far more control, but we're not covering it here because it can be very finicky in my experience.

Also, be very, very careful using either multiple numbered lists in a large document or using numbered lists where there are large gaps between the entries.

It's possible to do and I have certainly done so more than once. But this is one of those areas where I have wasted more time and energy than I can count going back and forth between different sections of a document to make sure that a change on page 10 didn't renumber my entries on page 65 or vice versa.

This may be more of an issue with Multilevel Lists, but it's definitely something to watch for. At the very end, when you are done making all other edits, if you are using numbered lists, make sure that you walk through your document from start to finish to confirm that all of the lists are working as expected.

To remove numbering, select your entries and then click on the numbering option once more.

The mini formatting menu also includes a Numbering dropdown menu.

Page and Document Formatting

Okay, that was the paragraph level. Now on to the page and document level. I'm not going to cover everything here, just the basics you need to get started.

Headers and Footers

You can insert text into the header or footer of your document. This is text that is kept separate from the main body of your document. The header is the text at the top of the document, the footer is the text at the bottom.

Often, for example, on a multi-page report you will want to have a header that states the title of the report and maybe the author of the report. Or maybe you want to include a corporate logo on the top of every page.

And usually you'll want a page number in the footer of the document. (Page numbers are covered specifically in the next section.)

To insert a header or footer go to the Header & Footer section of the Insert tab and then click on the dropdown arrow for the one you want. Word will give you a series of choices, some of which are very fancy:

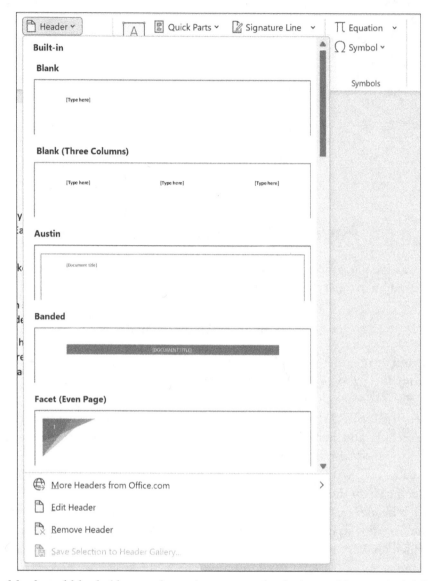

The top two, blank and blank (three columns), are generic choices with no special formatting that allow you to provide your own text in the spots that say [Text here].

The ones below that are fancier. You can also go to the web for even more choices using the Office.com option below the list of built-in choices. The ones that use [Author Name] or [Document Title] are going to pull in properties of the document to populate those particular fields, so be wary of using those.

If you choose one of the blank options it will insert text fields that say [Type here] that you then can click on and delete or replace with text. Here I've entered text for the first of the three-part footer option:

Footer		
Really Important Report	[Type here]	[Type here]

The Insert section of the Header & Footer tab includes options to insert Date & Time information, document information such as Author, File Name, File Path, and Document Title, or pictures. I had one employer where we would regularly insert the corporate logo in the header, for example.

The Options section of the Header & Footer tab also includes checkboxes for if you want a different header or footer for the first page or different header or footer for odd and even pages. I use these often because I usually need to have a different header for the first page of the document since a first-page header usually doesn't include text.

To return to your document from your header or footer, double-click back onto the text of your document or use the Esc key. You can also click on the Close Header and Footer option in the Header & Footer tab.

To return to the header or footer, just double-click on the header or footer text. You can also right-click on that text and choose Edit Header or Edit Footer, whichever option appears. This second option works even when there is no text in that header or footer.

Now let's talk about page numbering.

Page Numbering

First, if you already have a text-based header or footer that you've inserted, you can click into the header or footer and then go to the Page Number dropdown in the Header & Footer section of the Header & Footer tab and choose Current Position to insert a page number there. The top option in the secondary dropdown menu will insert a basic page number, but there are other options shown below that.

If you don't already have a header or footer in your document and you want to insert a page number, go to the Header & Footer section of the Insert tab and click on the Page Number dropdown arrow to see a list of options that include Top of Page, Bottom of Page, Page Margins, and Current Position.

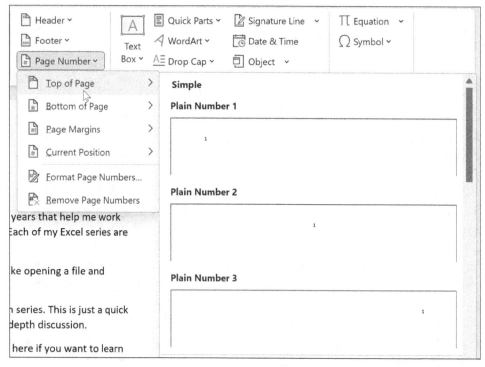

These are all locations where you can place that page number. Top of page, bottom of page, etc. And each has a secondary dropdown menu that will provide a number of options to choose from as you can see above for Top of Page.

Be sure to use the scroll bars to see the full range of choices. You can't preview the choices in your actual document, but when you click on a choice it will be inserted and formatted based on your choice. You'll also see that the header, footer, etc. section is now the section of the document that you're working in:

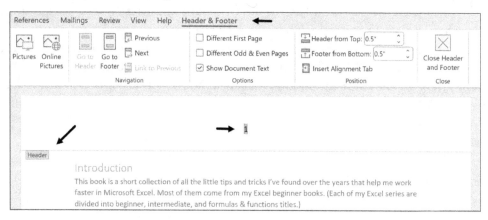

In the Header & Footer section in the far left-hand side of the Header & Footer tab is a Page Number dropdown. You can click on that and select Format Page Numbers to bring up the Page Number Format dialogue box:

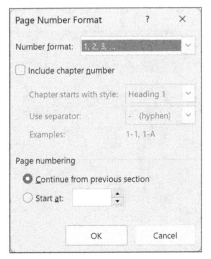

This will allow you to choose a number format (1, 2, 3 vs. i, ii, iii) for your pages as well as, if needed, restart the page numbering of your document.

For example, if you have a ten-page document but the first four pages are a cover page and introductory information you may want to have page numbering start on page five but with the number 1. You can do that using this dialogue box.

For the purposes of this book, that's as deep as we're going to go with this one, but know that you can use section breaks to have different headers and footers in different sections of your document if needed. So you could have those first five pages numbered i, ii, iii and then the main body of your document numbered 1, 2, 3, etc. But that requires section breaks which are covered in the next book in this series.

To exit where you inserted your page number, double-click back onto the text of your document or use the Esc key. You can also click on the Close Header and Footer option in the Header & Footer tab.

To return to editing your page number, right-click on where the page number is and choose Edit Header or Edit Footer, whichever option appears. If you put a page number into the margins, you will likely need to right-click where the header or footer would go to get back to editing that page number.

Another option is to double-click on the page number to re-open the header or footer, but for page numbers I find that unreliable.

Page Orientation

By default documents in Word are in Portrait orientation, meaning that the longer edge of the page is on the side and the shorter edge is along the top of the page. If you ever need to change that so that the longer edge is along the top, then the way to do that is to set the document orientation to Landscape.

One way to do this is using the Orientation dropdown in the Page Setup section of the Layout tab:

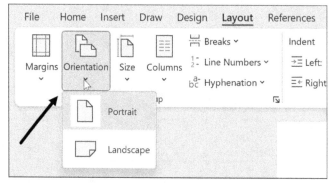

You can also do this when you go to print your document, but if I'm going to do this I usually prefer to set it that way before I start entering text and formatting.

Margins

The same goes for margins. Usually if I'm going to change those from their default I want to do so at the start not the end.

The Margins dropdown is also located in the Page Setup section of the Layout tab. Click on the dropdown arrow to see your available default choices:

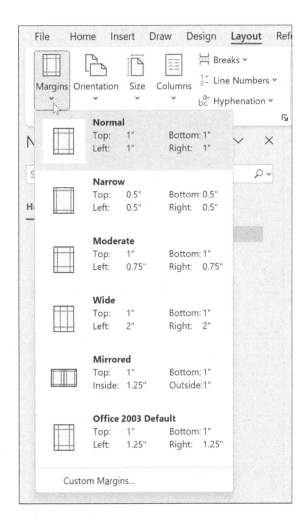

The Normal margin layout as of January 2023 is 1" on all sides, but there are options for Narrow, Moderate, Wide, Mirrored, and Office 2003 Default in that list. You can also completely customize your margins using the Custom Margins option at the bottom.

Paper Size

Another one you may want to change before you get started is the setting for the paper size you're going to use. This too is in the Page Setup section of the Layout tab under Size. Click on the dropdown arrow to see your available choices and then choose the one you want.

When you do so the page displayed in the main workspace will change to reflect your chosen paper size.

Other Basic Word Functionality

Real quick before we cover printing, I want to cover some other basic Word functionality like find and replace and zoom.

Zoom

By default I believe Word documents display at a 100% zoom level. That means that what you see on the screen is the same size as the text will be when it prints. But sometimes you may want what you see on the screen to be bigger or to be smaller.

You can make that happen by using Zoom. Now, to be clear, zoom only impacts your document. All of your menu options will stay the same size. To zoom your menu options you need to change your Windows settings.

So this is only for zooming in or out on the document you're working on.

The easiest way to do this is to use the slider in the bottom right corner:

You can left-click and drag that bar that is positioned along the line that shows a minus sign at one end and a plus sign at the other. The amount to which you are currently zoomed will show on the right-hand side. As you move to the right the text in your document will become larger. As you move to the left it will become smaller and you'll be able to see more of the document than you could before.

You can also just click on the line to either side of that bar. I find clicking and dragging allows me a little bit more control over the level to which I zoom.

There are also Zoom options in the Zoom section of the View tab.

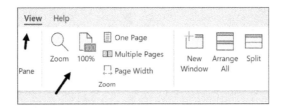

I use the 100% option there to return my view to 100% because it's easier to get that exact value that way than to click around on the slider.

Click on Zoom to open the Zoom dialogue box which will give you pre-populated choices of 75%, 100%, or 200%. You can also enter a custom percentage.

The dialogue box also has options for zoom to page width, text width, whole page, and many pages.

The One Page option zooms out so you can see one single page on the screen. The Multiple Pages option shows two pages on the screen. The Page Width option zooms in so that the document covers the entire width of the workspace.

If you need this, play around with it to find the setting that works for you.

Views

It's generally best in my opinion to leave Word on its default view setting which is Print Layout. That's where you can see gray space on the sides and the document looks the way it will when it prints. But in the View tab there is a Views section that includes other options.

Read Mode hides your ribbon up top and shows two pages side by side with no gray space around them:

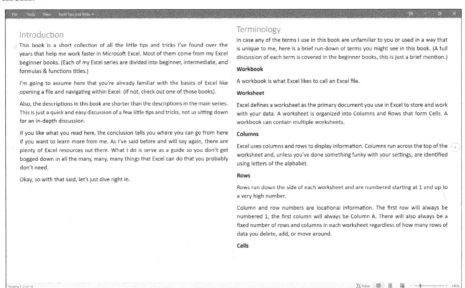

Use Esc to get out of it and go back to the Print Layout view.

Web Layout shows how your document would look as a webpage. It basically makes the document as wide as the entire workspace.

Outline shows your document in a bulleted outline format where each paragraph is displayed like an item in a bulleted list.

Draft shows just the text in the document not any objects.

I only bring Views up here because sometimes a document will get into one of these modes and you need to know how to get it back to the view you're used to. So if that happens to you, try Esc, Close [X View] option in the top menu, or change your view in the Views section of the View tab to Print Layout.

Find

Find and Replace are incredibly useful tools, but you have to be careful with Replace, so I'm going to cover Find first.

By default you should have a Navigation task pane open on the left-hand side of your workspace. If you do, click on Results below the search bar.

If you don't, use Ctrl + F to open it. It should look like this and if you used Ctrl + F your cursor should appear in the search bar already:

If you want to find text, just type the text you're looking for into that search bar, and hit Enter.

You should see a listing of results appear below that with snippets of the text surrounding each result, like here where I searched for shortcut and there were three results, one a chapter header and two that were part of paragraphs:

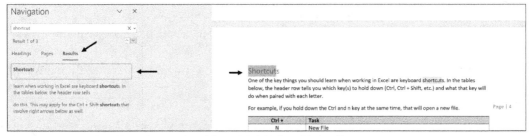

In the document itself each result will be highlighted in yellow.

In the Navigation task pane, you can either click on a specific result to go to that point in your document or you can use the up and down arrows on the right-hand side that are located just below the search bar to move between search results.

Using the search field works just fine for a basic text search.

But if you need something more advanced than that, X out your search term, and then click on the magnifying glass at the end of the search bar to choose a search type:

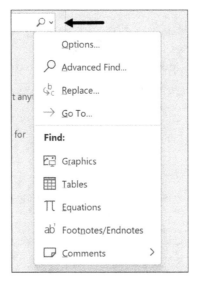

The Advanced Find option will open the Find and Replace dialogue box to the Find tab.

Click on More to see your advanced options:

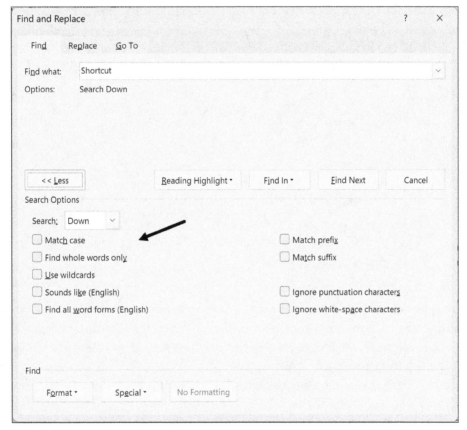

The two advanced options I use the most (and more so for Replace than Find, but we'll get there in a minute) are Match Case and Find Whole Words Only.

Match Case will only look for words that have the exact same capitalization as your search term. So if I want to look for "Word" as in Microsoft Word I would check that box so that the search doesn't return every use of "word", "foreword", etc.

Find Whole Words Only is another one that's very useful when there can be a lot of extraneous results. If I were to search for "excel" checking that box would keep Word from returning results for "excellent", "excellence", etc.

As you can see, there are other options there, too, so that you can find variations on a word with just that one search.

Down at the bottom are dropdowns for Format and Special. The Special dropdown lets you search for things like Paragraph Marks and Tab Characters. This can make fixing a poorly-formatted document much easier. If someone used paragraph marks to force the start of a new chapter in a document, for example, you can search and replace those paragraph marks with nothing. We'll cover that in a moment.

The Format dropdown has options for Font, Paragraph, Tabs, Language, Frame, Style, and Highlight. But usually I don't need that because I'm looking for simple formatting like all text in italics or all text in bold.

To search for all text in italics, go back to the Find What field, delete any text in that field, and then use Ctrl + I in that field. You should see a listing for Format appear that says Font: Italic.

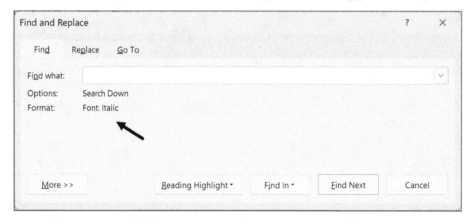

From there just click on Find Next to walk through and find all examples of italicized text.

Now. One warning here. You need to turn that off when you're done because Word will store that in the background and if you later try to do a simple search it will still be hanging on to that restriction to search for italicized text.

The way to turn that off is to just use Ctrl + I two more times in that Find What field to change it from Italic to Not Italic to off.

Replace

Now let's talk about Replace. Use Ctrl + H to open the Find and Replace dialogue box to the Replace tab.

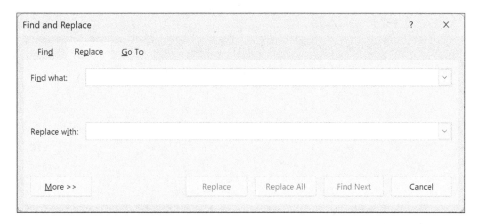

At its most basic what replace does is looks for the text you provide it in the Find What field and then replaces that text with the text you provide in the Replace With field.

Easy enough, right? Except…

It's very easy to mess up. Think of my example above where I want to find Excel. Let's say I just type that into the Find What field and say to replace with Word. Word will walk through the document and faithfully replace every instance of excel or Excel with Word. So I will end up with Wordlence instead of excellence and "the power to Word" instead of "the power to excel". Etc.

If you don't constrain the search portion properly you can have some truly horrible results. That's why using Match Case and Find Whole Words only on the Replace side of things is crucial most times.

Also, unless you're very confident that you won't have any issues like that it can be a best practice to walk through and use Find Next and then the Replace button instead of using the Replace All button so that you replace your entries one at a time and can verify that you won't replace something you shouldn't.

If you ever have something you need to delete, like extra enters in a document, just leave the Replace With field empty when you find and replace and that will have the effect of deleting what you searched for.

Word Count

In the Proofing section of the Review tab there is a Word Count option that will give you the number of pages, words, characters (no spaces), characters (with spaces), paragraphs, and lines in your document.

If you just need the number of words in the document, it's displayed in the bottom left corner. If you select a subset of your text, it will also display the number of words in your selected text as well.

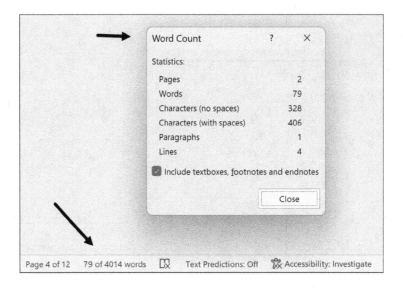

Show Paragraph Formatting

Sometimes I need to be able to see all of the little formatting marks in my text, like the paragraph marks and whether someone used spaces, the Tab key, or formatting to indent a paragraph. To see all of that, click on the little paragraph mark in the Paragraph section of the Home tab. It's on the top row on the far end. You can also use Ctrl + Shift + 8 to turn it on or off.

This is also useful for showing any page or section breaks in a document so we'll revisit it again in the intermediate book but just wanted to mention it quickly here.

Return to Last Place in Document

When you open a document you've been working on in Word, you should see on the right-hand side of the workspace towards the bottom, a pop-up box that asks if you want to return to where you were when you last closed the document.

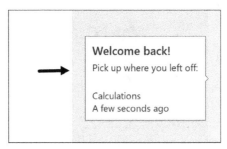

This can be incredibly useful when you're working on a longer document because it saves you having to scroll through 50+ pages to get back to where you were.

Just click on that image to go to your last location in the document.

This also, of course, means that you should give some thought to where your cursor is when you close out a document. For example, if I need to format the chapter headers in my document before I close it, I can do that, but then it's helpful to click back to the place I want to be when the document reopens so this can work for me.

If you don't catch the message right away, it will turn into a little flag off to the side. You

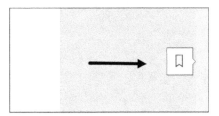

can still click on that to go to the last point in your document.

(If you hold your mouse over it, you'll see that welcome message again.)

Printing

Printing a document in Word is usually pretty straight-forward. (Nothing like printing in Excel.) The reason for that is because you can usually see exactly what the document is going to look like when printed as you're typing. If you're working in the Print Layout view, the document you're working on has your headers and footers and is the size and orientation it will be when printed.

Still. There are a number of printing options available that we should cover.

To print use Ctrl + P or go to File and then click on Print in the left-hand set of options. Both will take you to the Print screen:

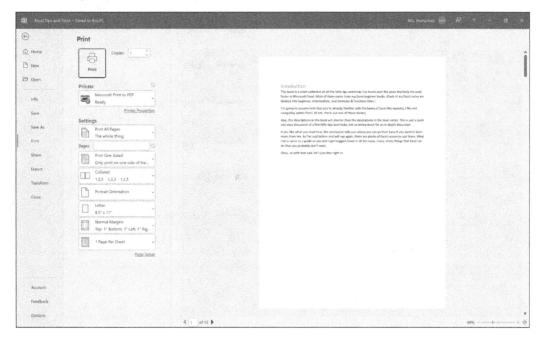

On the right-hand side is a preview of your document. You can see at the bottom of that space on the left-hand side the total number of pages and also which page of that total that you're currently viewing. There is a scroll bar on the right-hand side that you can use to move through the document or you can use those arrows down there by the number of pages.

On the left of that space is the print icon as well as all of your print choices. Let's look closer at those now:

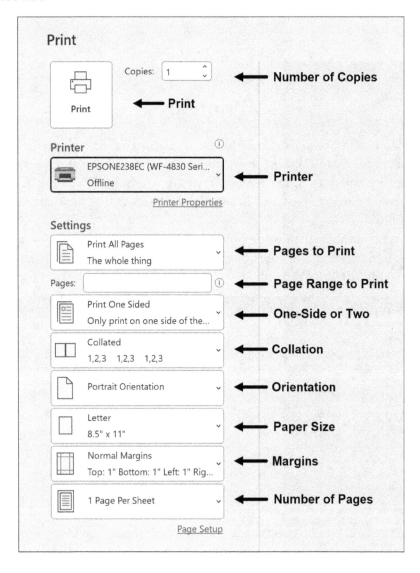

Print

At the very top on the left you can see a picture of a printer with the word Print underneath. That's what you click on when you're ready to print.

Copies

To the right of that is a white field labeled Copies. You can either click into that field and type a number or use the up and down arrows on the right-hand side to specify how many copies of the document to print.

Printer

Below that is where you tell Word what printer to use. Click on the dropdown arrow to see the list of available printers. You will also likely see a Microsoft Print to PDF option that will let you create a PDF version of the document. (I usually Save As a PDF instead.) Microsoft XPS Document Writer does something similar, but may not be as accessible to all other users as PDF.

At the bottom of the list you can add a printer if the one you want is not listed.

I will note here that a year or two ago I noticed that my Word and Excel programs were getting hung up. I want to say that they wouldn't close without a significant delay. I did some research and it turned out it was something to do with having my printer listed as the default printer. The issue went away when I changed the default printer to Microsoft Print to PDF. So if you ever experience that issue, maybe try that as a solution. You can always choose your printer from the list when you're ready to print.

Print All Pages / Print Selection / Print Current Page / Custom Print

Leave this on Print All Pages if you want to print the entire document. Print Selection will only be available if you selected text or objects within the document before choosing to print. Print Current Page will print whatever page you currently have visible in the print preview section. Custom Print uses the page range typed below that dropdown.

This dropdown also lets you print your document information, a list of tracked changes in the document, a list of styles used in the document, a list of items in the AutoText gallery, or a list of your custom shortcut keys.

You can also choose here whether to print the document with markup or not if you were using track changes.

And at the bottom of the dropdown you can choose to print only odd pages or only even pages.

Pages

If there are specific page numbers that you want to print instead of the whole document, you can enter those values in the white field next to where it says Pages. To print a page range write the first page number of the range and then a hyphen and then the last number of the range. You can also list multiple page numbers or ranges using a comma to separate each number or number range.

Hold your mouse over the small i next to that field for examples.

Print One Sided / Print on Both Sides (Long Edge) / Print on Both Sides (Short Edge) / Manually Print on Both Sides

If your printer can do so, you can choose to print on both sides of the page. If you do so, flipping on the long edge works best (in my opinion) for when you're using Portrait orientation and flipping on the short edge works best for when you're using Landscape.

Collated / Uncollated

This setting only matters when you're printing more than one copy of a document that is more than one page long. Your choices are to print all of page 1 first then all of page 2 then all of page 3, etc. Or to print one full copy of the document and then another full copy of the document and then another until all copies are done.

Collated is when you print one full copy at a time. Uncollated is when you print all of page 1 then all of page 2, etc.

Portrait Orientation / Landscape Orientation

We discussed the difference between these previously. Usually you should make this decision before you're ready to print your document so that you can see what the document will actually look like as you're writing it. But as a reminder, portrait is what a standard school report generally looks like with the long edge of the page on the side. Landscape is more what a PowerPoint presentation looks like with the long edge along the top.

Letter / A4 / Japan LPhoto / Etc.

This is the dropdown where you can choose which paper size to print to. Again, you should probably set this before you start to write, but I have had situations where I was in the UK and needed to switch to A4 at the last moment, so it does happen that you make this choice at the very end.

Normal Margins / Narrow Margins / Moderate Margins / Wide Margins / Mirrored Margins / Office 2003 Default

This is where you can set the margins for your document, but again, one that should probably be set at the start not the end.

1 Page Per Sheet / 2 Pages Per Sheet / 4 Pages Per Sheet / 6 Pages Per Sheet / 8 Pages Per Sheet / 16 Pages Per Sheet

This allows you to print more than one page of your document on a single sheet of paper. If you ever had a final exam where the professor told you that you could bring one page of notes, you may have tried this option. You know, write 16 pages of notes and then cram them all onto one page by printing it really small.

It's also sometimes useful for saving paper if you're doing a quick review of a report or document and don't need to see the text at full size.

Page Setup

Opens the Page Setup dialogue box, but it doesn't really give you any options that you haven't already addressed elsewhere.

Customize Settings

We touched on this briefly with the Theme setting and with AutoCorrect and a few other places, but before we wrap up I wanted to revisit how to customize your settings. Because as time goes on Office seems to add more and more, for lack of a better word, crap that's the default. Some of it raises privacy concerns, some of it is just not the way I prefer to work.

Now, I will say that the more you customize your version of Word the more you may get tripped up while working with someone else's version. But at this point I think it's kind of essential to know some of these settings.

So. First, go to File and then click on Options at the very bottom of the screen on the left-hand side. This will open the Word Options dialogue box to the General tab.

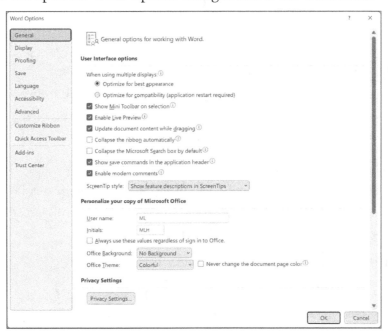

I suggest you scroll through all of these sections to see if there's anything there that you don't want. Or that you do. But I'm going to point out a few here.

General

- Enable or disable the Mini Toolbar
- Enable or disable Live Preview of a potential change
- Change your user name and initials for track changes
- Change your Office Theme
- Enable or disable LinkedIn features in your Office applications
- Enable or disable showing the Start screen when Word opens
- Use Privacy Settings to turn on or off connected experiences
- Enable or disable new style of track changes (this one looks like it's only temporary)

Display

- Enable or disable showing white space between pages in Print Layout view (if you don't do this all the pages run together like they're one long page.)
- Choose formatting marks that are always visible on the screen

Proofing

- Customize AutoCorrect Options
- Enable or disable various spelling and grammar check settings
- Enable or disable showing readability statistics when you ask for word count

Save

- Set timing for AutoRecover save
- Set where documents save by default (can save to computer instead of OneDrive)

Advanced

- Enable or disable default of select to select an entire word
- Set a default paragraph style
- Enable or disable text predictions while typing

- Set default settings for pasting text
- Set how images are or are not compressed when added to a document and the default resolution
- Set the number of Recent Documents and Recent Folders to list
- Enable or disable scroll bars

Customize Ribbon

Allows you to add or delete the items that are in each tab at the top of the screen. Be VERY CAREFUL in customizing this because it will make it more difficult to use other versions of Word either on someone else's computer or at a new employer or school.

Quick Access Toolbar

Allows you to add tasks that you perform frequently that you want to always have available regardless of the tab you're working in. For me, I usually have the options for Insert Page Break and Read Aloud up there because I use them often enough and they are not located in the Home tab and I don't want to go find them.

Click on the option you want and then use Add to move it to the Quick Access Toolbar and then be sure to click on Show Quick Access Toolbar at the bottom of the screen so it actually appears for you.

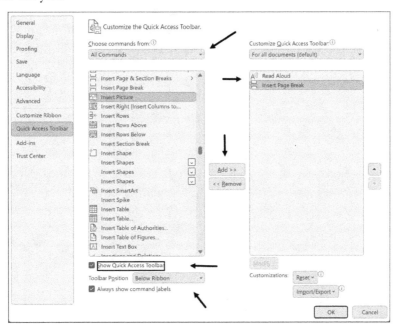

When you do that you'll have an option to show the Quick Access Toolbar either above the ribbon or below it. I actually prefer above so that it's next to that save icon. Here is what that looks like with Read Aloud and Insert Page Break added:

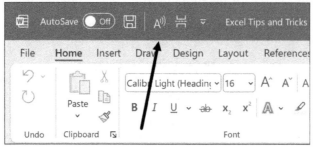

Trust Center

Opens the Trust Center dialogue box which contains a number of settings related to privacy and trust. The Privacy Options screen includes a Document Inspector that will review your document for any information that may not be visible but that you may want to remove before sharing.

Just be careful if you're using track changes that you don't remove user information unless it's really the final version of the document. If you remove user information and then continue to work on a document with a team, all edits from that point forward will simply be listed as edits by Author and you won't be able to see who did what.

That page also has a check box where you can enable warning before saving or sending a file that has track changes or comments in it. (Something that you may want to do if you use track changes since I have on occasion been on the receiving end of a "final" document that still had comments and track changes in it which made for a very interesting read.)

Conclusion

Okay, so that's the end of our introduction to Microsoft Word. There's a lot more that you can do in Word like use Text Styles to apply formatting, build tables, track changes, and use sections to apply different page formatting to different parts of a document. But for basic day-to-day use this should've been a solid introduction that will let you write a report or letter and format it properly.

From here, there are a few directions you can go. You can continue learning with me and move on to *Intermediate Word 365* which will cover the next level of information.

I don't have some exclusive super-secret insight, but what I do provide is a path forward so that you don't get lost trying to learn everything. Also, I sometimes provide opinions on certain things based on my corporate and educational experiences that a straight read of the help text won't give.

But you can learn as needed using Microsoft's Help function and website or by finding various blogs and tutorials online.

For Word's help, go to the Help tab and then click on Help.

A task pane will appear on the right-hand side where you can then search for what you need. It does require internet access.

With a number of tasks in the top menu tabs you can also hold your mouse over the task and there will be a description of what it does. Some tasks have a Tell Me More option that you can click on to open the Help screen for that specific task, like here for Format Painter:

I'd say don't be afraid to try different things and see how they work. Ctrl + Z, Undo, is your friend if you do something that doesn't look right. Also, click around to the different tabs and see the options you have.

And if something I discussed was confusing or you can't find an answer, reach out to me. I'm happy to help and point you in the right direction.

Okay then. I hope this gave you a strong foundation to build from. Good luck with it. You can do this.

Control Shortcuts

Letter	Task
1	Single-Space
2	Double-Space
A	Select All
B	Bold
C	Copy
E	Center
F	Find
H	Replace
I	Italicize
J	Justify
L	Align Left
N	New File
P	Print Screen
R	Align Right
S	Save
U	Underline
V	Paste
X	Cut
Y	Redo
Z	Undo

Intermediate
Word 365

WORD 365 ESSENTIALS - BOOK 2

M.L. HUMPHREY

CONTENTS

CONTENTS (CONT.)

Introduction

In *Word 365 for Beginners* we covered the basics of Microsoft Word including text, paragraph, and page formatting; numbered lists; bulleted lists; and printing. But there's a lot more you can do in Word and that's what this book is for, to take your use of Word to the next level.

The key topics we're going to cover here are Styles, Page and Section Breaks, Multilevel Lists, Tables, and Track Changes. We'll also revisit headers and footers briefly and cover some minor topics such as inserting symbols, footnotes, and watermarks. It won't be everything you can do in Word, but it will cover a substantial part of it.

This book is written using Word 365 as it exists in January 2023 and written using the desktop version of the program. All screenshots use the Colorful Theme.

Okay, then, let's just dive right in with one of my favorite little tricks to use in Word: Styles. But first, a quick recap of basic terminology so you know what I mean when I say things.

Basic Terminology Recap

These terms were covered in detail in *Word 365 for Beginners*. This is just meant as a refresher.

Tab

When I refer to a tab, I am referring to the menu options at the top of the screen. The tab options that are available by default are File, Home, Insert, Draw, Design, Layout, References, Mailings, Review, View, and Help, but for certain tasks additional tabs will appear.

Click

If I tell you to click on something, that means to move your cursor over to that location and then either right-click or left-click. If I don't say which to do, left-click.

Left-Click / Right-Click

A left-click is generally for selecting something and involves using the left-hand side of your mouse or bottom left-hand corner of your trackpad. A right-click is generally for opening a dropdown menu and involves using the right-hand side of your mouse or bottom right-hand corner of your trackpad.

Left-Click and Drag

Left-click and drag means to left-click and then hold that left-click as you move your mouse.

Dropdown Menu

A dropdown menu is a list of choices that you can view by right-clicking in a specific spot or clicking on an arrow next to or below one of the available choices under the tabs up top. Depending on where you are in the workspace, a dropdown menu may actually drop upward from that spot.

Expansion Arrow

In the bottom right corner of some of the sections under the tabs in the top menu you will see an arrow, which I refer to as an expansion arrow. Clicking on an expansion arrow will usually open a dialogue box or task pane and is often the way to see the largest number of options.

Dialogue Box

A dialogue box is a pop-up box that will open on top of your workspace and will usually include the largest number of choices for that particular setting or task.

Scroll Bar

Scroll bars appear when there are more options than can appear on the screen or when your document is longer than will show on the screen. They can be used to move through the remainder of the choices or document.

Task Pane

A task pane is a set of additional options that will appear to the sides or even below the main workspace. The Navigation pane is by default visible on the left-hand side of the workspace. You can close a task pane by clicking on the X in the top right corner of the pane.

Control Shortcuts

Control shortcuts are shortcuts that let you perform certain tasks in Word. I will write them as Ctrl + and then a character. That means to hold down both the Ctrl key and that character. So Ctrl + C means hold down Ctrl and C, which will let you copy your selection. Even though I will write each shortcut using a capital letter it doesn't have to be the capitalized version to work.

Styles

If you're going to do any formatting in Word, using styles will save you a tremendous amount of time and effort.

For example, the first print books I ever formatted I used Word. And I was able to set up three styles that I could use, one for the chapter names, one for the first paragraph of a chapter or section, and one for all other paragraphs. It was then a very simple matter to apply the "all other paragraphs" format to my entire document and then go through and for each chapter header and each first paragraph in a chapter or section apply the other formats.

That easily let me create a document with consistent formatting throughout.

A style has the font, font size, color, paragraph spacing, paragraph indent, etc. all built in, so you don't have to keep changing those settings. It's much better at ensuring consistency of appearance than trying to format your paragraphs manually. And much easier to apply than the Format Painter option.

Also, you can create shortcuts for your styles so that you don't even have to use your mouse, you can just use your keyboard shortcut to apply each style.

Alright. Let's walk through how to use them now.

Styles are located in the Styles section of the Home tab:

The number of styles that are visible by default will depend on your screen size, but usually it will be a handful or so. There is a downward-pointing arrow on the right-hand side of that listing (see the screenshot above) that you can click on to expand the list of styles. If you do so, it will look something like this:

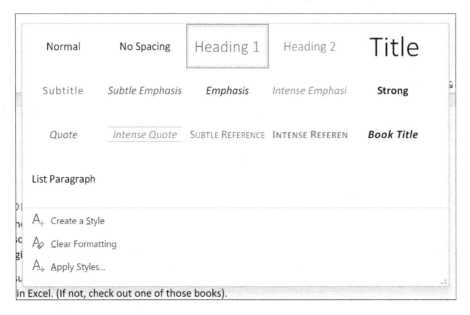

Those are all of the default styles that Word uses. Each one is formatted to show a bit of what that style will look like if applied to your text.

When I'm drafting a document like this one, I usually have my paragraphs use the Normal style and my chapters use the Heading 1 style. I then change the styles when I'm done and ready to format.

The Normal style will be applied to your text by default so you don't have to do anything to use it. But the Heading 1 style does have to be applied.

To apply a style to your text, click onto that paragraph or line of text. (You don't have to select all of the text, just click onto some portion of that paragraph or line of text.) Next, click on the style you want from the Style listing in the Styles section of the Home tab.

The Normal and Heading styles can also be applied using a control shortcut. Ctrl + Shift + N will apply the Normal style. Ctrl + Alt + 1 will apply Heading 1, Ctrl + Alt + 2 will apply Heading 2, and Ctrl + Alt + 3 will apply Heading 3.

If you use the Heading styles, Word will also show any text with those styles applied in your Navigation pane on the left-hand side under the Headings view. Here you can see my chapter names, Introduction, Terminology, Shortcuts, etc. from *Excel Tips and Tricks*, all of which were formatted using the Heading 1 style:

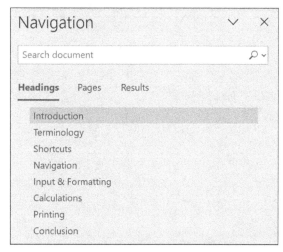

Click on each of those entries to go to that part of your document.

You can also left-click and drag one of those entries in that list to move the entire section to a new location in your document. The text that moves will be all text from that header through to the next text in the document that has that same heading style or a higher-level heading style.

Meaning, that if I have applied the Heading 1 style to all of my chapter titles and I left-click and drag one of my chapter titles to a new location in the list, that will move that entire chapter to the new location. But it will leave all subsequent chapters where they are.

Here, for example, I dragged Conclusion to the top above Introduction, which you can see on the left-hand-side listing. You can also see by looking at the document that all text from the chapter moved, too:

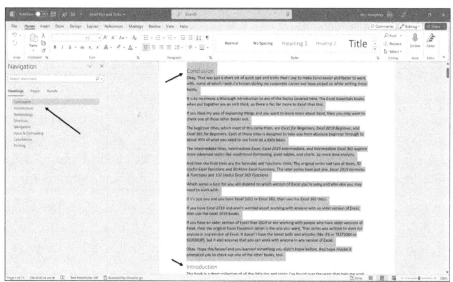

Here is an example where I've applied the Heading 2 style to the chapter sub-sections, Pin a File and Navigate Between Worksheets:

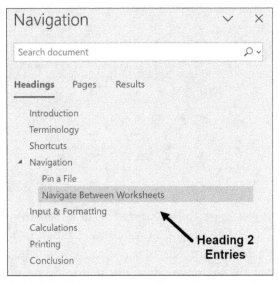

If I click and drag one of the Heading 2 entries, all text between that entry and the next listed heading will move. So if I move Pin a File, all text from there to Navigate Between Worksheets will move. But if I move Navigate Between Worksheets, all text from there to the next chapter, Input & Formatting, will move.

I know that sounds very complex, but if you need to do this, the best way to learn is to try it out and see what happens. I very rarely need to click and drag to move an entire section of my document, but it does sometimes happen. If the idea of doing so using the Headings listing scares you, there's always cut and paste.

Also, when you use a Heading level, like I did here with Heading 2, Word will automatically make the next heading level, in this case, Heading 3, available in the Styles section.

When you use the heading styles in your document, that also allows you to collapse those sections so the text under that heading is hidden, like I've done here for Pin a File:

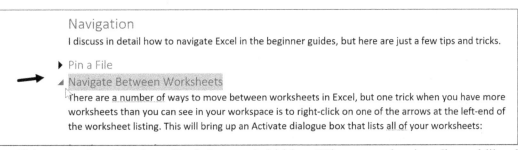

You still have the heading, but all of the text is hidden. When a section is collapsed like that, the black arrow to the left of the heading will be visible. Click on that to expand the section once more.

To collapse a section, you need to hold your mouse over the header to make that blue arrow appear on the left-hand side like I've done above for Navigate Between Worksheets. Click on that arrow to collapse the section and hide the text.

Headings are useful when drafting a large document, but the default Word styles are usually not what I want to use for my final document, so once I'm done I need to create custom styles or apply styles from another document.

Let's walk through how to do that now.

First off, I'm not a fan of messing with the default styles. So I try to leave Normal and the Headings alone. I won't directly modify those if I can avoid it.

Instead, what I do is I take a paragraph and I modify it so that it's formatted the way I want.

(If I have another document that is already formatted properly I will use the Format Painter from the Clipboard section of the Home tab to bring in that formatting for me. Sometimes that also brings in a style name, too, and I don't have to do the rest of these steps to create a new style, I can just apply it where needed. But assuming it doesn't…)

Next, once my paragraph is formatted the way I want, I expand the Styles section and click on the option to Create a Style. That brings up the Create New Style From Formatting dialogue box:

I change the name of the style to something that I'll remember and then click OK. That adds that style as an option in the Styles section of the Home tab:

I can then click on that option to format any other paragraph in my document using that style. (We'll talk in a moment about how to do this quickly.)

If you want there to be a keyboard shortcut for that style, right-click on the style in the Styles section and choose Modify from the dropdown menu. That will open the Modify Style dialogue box. At the bottom of that dialogue box is a dropdown menu that says Format. Click on that to see a list of choices. The one you want is Shortcut Key:

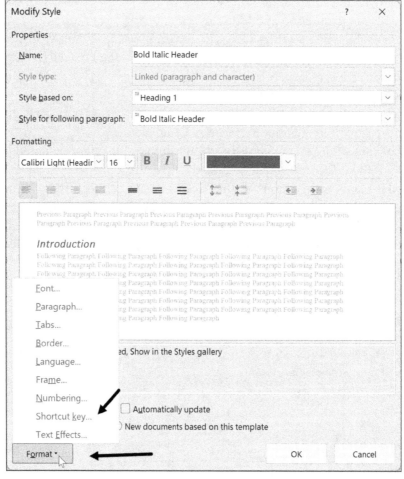

That will open a Customize Keyboard dialogue box where you can click into the Press New Shortcut Key field. Use the shortcut key combination you want and Word will populate it in that field. But watch out that the shortcut you come up with isn't already in use elsewhere. (Word will tell you if it is.)

Here I've assigned Ctrl + } to this style. Word shows that and also shows that it is currently not assigned to any other task:

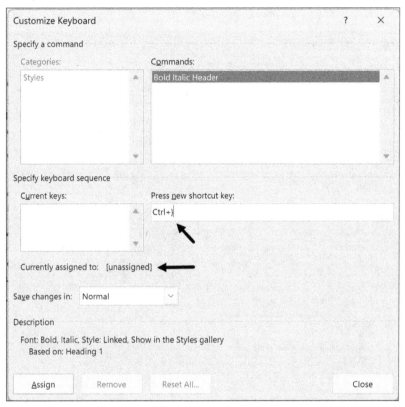

If I want to keep that as my shortcut I can then click on Assign and when I need that format I can apply it to any text in my document using the shortcut instead of having to go to the Style section up top. (It can save time to do this if you're applying styles as you move through a document, because a keyboard shortcut uses the keyboard whereas accessing the menus up top usually requires going to the mouse or trackpad.)

Often, though, what I do is I swap out all of my Normal-formatted paragraphs for paragraphs formatted in my custom style all at once. To do this, right-click on the Normal style option and choose Select All:

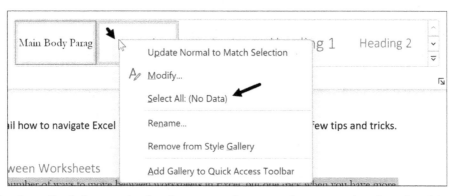

That will select all of the text in the document that uses the Normal style. Like this:

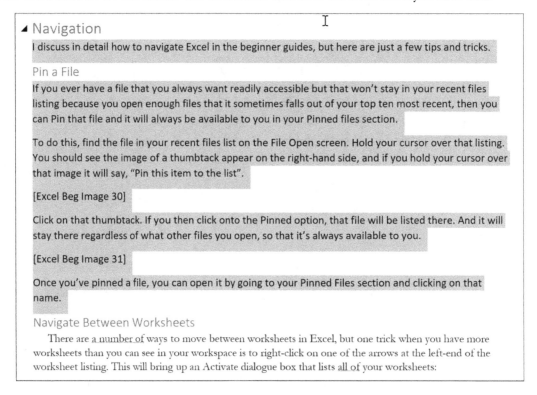

To change all of those Normal-style text entries over to a different style, select the new style from the Styles section. And done:

It only took about five seconds for Word to apply my new style to all of the paragraphs in my document that had used the Normal style previously. I could do the same for the Heading 1 and Heading 2 styles and then create a first paragraph style that uses a control shortcut and go through and manually apply that one.

A very easy way to format a document.

If you realize that your text style is not formatted the way you want, edit one paragraph of text that uses that style and then right-click on the style name at the top of the workspace and choose Update [Style Name] to Match Selection.

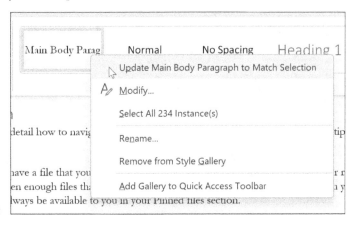

That will change all text entries in your document that use that style.

I find that easier than right-clicking on the style and choosing the Modify option which will open a Modify Style dialogue box where you can change any text or paragraph settings. It works, but it's easier for me to use the Paragraph and Font sections of the Home tab to modify a paragraph instead and then apply my changes that way.

Clicking on the expansion arrow for Styles will open a Styles floating task pane. You can click on Options there to open the Style Pane Options dialogue box which lets you control which styles are shown in the menu as well as a few other settings:

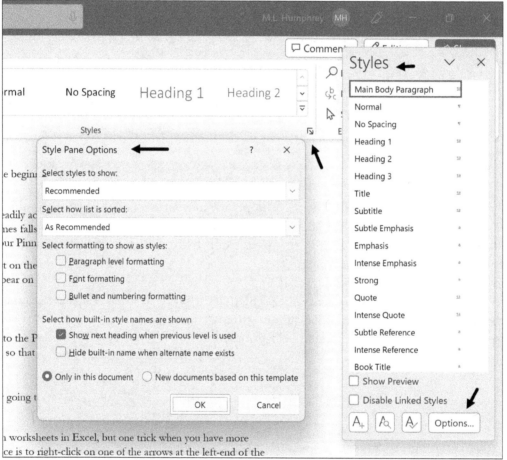

One final note. Every once in a while when I'm working with Heading 1 styles, Word will try to apply them to the paragraph above the chapter name. It's pretty obvious when it happens because you can see the text of that paragraph in the Headings section of the Navigation pane. If that ever happens to you, go to that paragraph, use Enter at the end of the paragraph and then apply the Normal style to it. The chapter name should keep the Heading 1 format, but it won't apply to that paragraph anymore.

And that's it. Pretty simple, but incredibly powerful. You should always use styles that incorporate paragraph formatting and indents instead of trying to use Enters, spaces, and the Tab key to format your text. Trust me on this.

Okay. On to a simple topic now, how to add a watermark to a document.

Watermarks

A watermark is text that appears in the background of a document. It's often light gray in color and says something like "Draft". Watermarks are useful for when you're circulating a document but want to make clear something about that document, like its incomplete status.

To add a watermark to your document, go to the Page Background section of the Design tab and click on the dropdown arrow under Watermark:

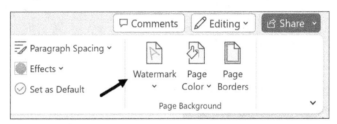

The dropdown will give you a few default choices that say CONFIDENTIAL, DO NOT COPY, DRAFT, or SAMPLE. Here are three of those examples:

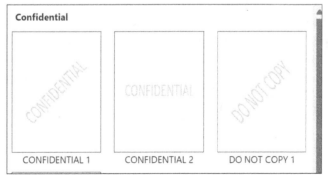

If that works for you, click on the option you want and you're done. The watermark will appear behind your text like this:

To do this, find the file in your recent files list on the File Open screen. Hold your cursor over that listing. You should see the image of a thumbtack appear on the right-hand side, and if you hold your cursor over that image it will say, "Pin this item to the list".

[Excel Beg Image 30]

Click on that thumbtack. If you then click onto the Pinned option, that file will be listed there. And it will stay there regardless of what other files you open, so that it's always available to you.

[Excel Beg Image 31]

Once you've pinned a file, you can open it by going to your Pinned Files section and clicking on that name.

Navigate Between Worksheets

There are a number of ways to move between worksheets in Excel, but one trick when you have more worksheets than you can see in your workspace is to right-click on one of the arrows at the left-end of the worksheet listing. This will bring up an Activate dialogue box that lists all of your worksheets:

[Excel Beg Image 41]

From there click on the name of the worksheet you want and then click on OK and Excel will take you to that worksheet.

Turn Off Scroll Lock

On occasion I will find that navigating in Excel isn't working the way I'm used to. I arrow and things don't move like they should. When this happens, it's usually because Scroll Lock somehow was turned on. The way to turn it back off is to click on the Scroll Lock key on your keyboard.

Unfortunately, I haven't had a computer with a Scroll Lock key in probably a decade, so you have to open a virtual keyboard to do this. Use the Windows key (the one with four squares to the left of your spacebar) + Ctrl + O to open it.

(Another option is to go through your Start menu to Settings and search for keyboard there and then toggle the on-screen keyboard to on.)

The keyboard will appear on your screen and look something like this:

If you don't like those choices, there is an option at the bottom of the dropdown to find more watermarks on Office.com or you can choose Custom Watermark, which will open the Printed Watermark dialogue box.

There you can specify the text, the font, the size of the text, the font color, the transparency level, and the angle of the text. You can also add a picture as your watermark. For the text, there are more options available in that dropdown menu, but you can also click into the box and type your own text.

Here I've changed the watermark to M.L. HUMPHREY and changed the font and color:

To do this, find the file in your recent files list on the File Open screen. Hold your cursor over that listing. You should see the image of a thumbtack appear on the right-hand side, and if you hold your cursor over that image it will say, "Pin this item to the list".

[Excel Beg Image 30]

Click on that thumbtack. If you then click onto the Pinned option, that file will be listed there. And it will stay there regardless of what other files you open, so that it's always available to you.

[Excel Beg Image 31]

Once you've pinned a file, you can open it by going to your Pinned Files section and clicking on that name.

Navigate Between Worksheets

There are a number of ways to move between worksheets in Excel, but worksheets than you can see in your workspace is to right-click on one worksheet listing. This will bring up an Activate dialogue box that lists al

[Excel Beg Image 41]

From there click on the name of the worksheet you want and then click that worksheet.

Turn Off Scroll Lock

On occasion I will find that navigating in Excel isn't working the way I'r move like they should. When this happens, it's usually because Scroll Loc to turn it back off is to click on the Scroll Lock key on your keyboard.

Unfortunately, I haven't had a computer with a Scroll Lock key in probal virtual keyboard to do this. Use the Windows key (the one with four squ Ctrl + O to open it.

(Another option is to go through your Start menu to Settings and search the on-screen keyboard to on.)

The keyboard will appear on your screen and look something like this:

There is also a No Watermark option there, but the Remove Watermark option in the dropdown menu will also remove any watermark that's been added to a document.

If you need to modify an existing watermark, use the Custom Watermark option. You can also replace it by choosing one of the other pre-formatted options.

Page Breaks

It can be tempting to use Enter to move text to the next page when that's needed. Don't. As I've mentioned before and I'll mention again, manually trying to force formatting onto your text is a very, very bad idea. It creates a lot of unnecessary work and is very prone to breaking or having inconsistencies. One little change somewhere in your document and suddenly everything is off.

The way to move text to the next page and not have all those issues is to use a Page Break. To insert one, go to the point in your document where you want to insert the break and then go to the Pages section of the Insert tab and click on Page Break:

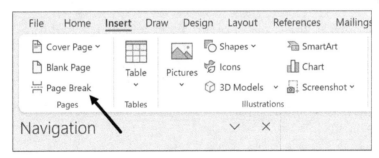

That will automatically move your cursor down to the next page in your document.

By default your page breaks in your document will not be visible. But if you click on the Show/Hide paragraph marks option in the Paragraph section of the Home tab, you can make them visible:

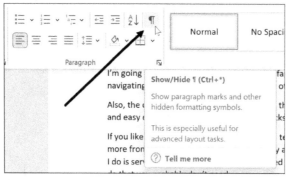

Here is an example of what that looks like:

In this case, the page break is on its own line. Sometimes that can be a problem because it forces a blank page that you don't want. If it is, you can click onto the line above and use Delete to bring the page break up to the last line of text.

If the last line of text is really long, sometimes you'll only see part of the text that identifies a page break:

To remove a page break, just treat it like any other text or paragraph mark and either use Delete or Backspace, depending on where you are relative to the break.

You can also find a page break option in the Page Setup section of the Layout tab under the Breaks dropdown menu:

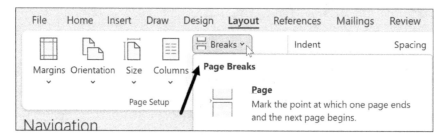

As I mentioned in *Word 365 for Beginners*, Page Break is actually a task that I add to my Quick Access Toolbar so that I don't have to go searching for it since I use it often enough and it's not on the Home tab.

Okay. Now let's discuss section breaks, which can also be found in that Breaks dropdown menu.

Section Breaks

Page breaks simply push text to the next page, but all of the formatting, document size, etc. remains the same. Section breaks, on the other hand, let you create different sections of your document that are formatted in different ways.

When might you need this?

If you are writing a report that has appendices that are landscape orientation instead of portrait orientation, you can achieve this in one single document by using section breaks between the main report and your appendices.

When I used to format print books using Word, I would use section breaks to have different headers and footers in different parts of my book.

So, for example, in the print version of this book you will see that the header for each chapter uses that chapter's name and that there is no header on the page that starts each chapter. The way to achieve that is to have different sections for each chapter.

Another place where that needs to happen is when you have a book that has all chapters starting on the right-hand page which sometimes requires a blank left-hand page. That can only be achieved if the blank page has different headers and footers compared to the other pages in the book.

Also, different sections are needed for any front matter, like tables of contents, which usually have separate page numbering from the main portion of the document.

* * *

Now that you understand what section breaks can be used for, let's look at your available options, which can be found in the Breaks dropdown in the Page Setup section of the Layout tab:

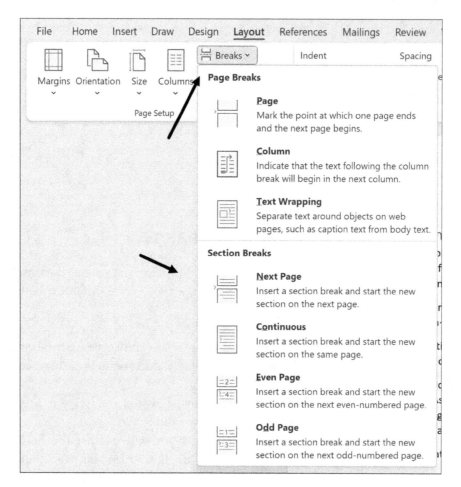

You have four choices there: Next Page, Continuous, Even Page, and Odd Page.

Continuous means that the break will happen on that same page. This could be used for a scenario where you have a single column of text at the top of the page and then multiple columns later in the page. Like this:

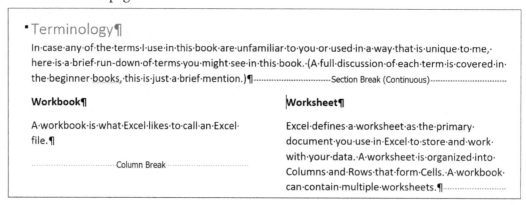

You can see here (maybe) that the first paragraph of that Terminology chapter is a single column. But then below that I have one column with the definition of Workbook next to another column with the definition for Worksheet. There is a Continuous Section Break between that first paragraph and the two definition columns.

When I selected that text and applied two-column formatting to it, Word automatically inserted the Section Break for me, which was nice, but I could have manually inserted it as well. (We'll come back to this more in the next chapter when we cover columns.)

The other three options, Next Page, Even Page, and Odd Page are all options that start a new section on another page. Just as their names imply, that other page is either the next one available, the next even-numbered page, or the next odd-numbered page.

For Even Page and Odd Page, Word will insert a blank page in between if needed.

Now, a warning here. I found in older versions of Word that when I tried to use the Odd Page Break, Word would accurately insert that particular section break, but it would somehow remove my previous odd-page section breaks from my document and turn them into next-page breaks instead.

I no longer use Word for book formatting and I wasn't able to replicate that issue today, so it may be fixed in Word 365 as of January 2023, but in case it isn't, Next Page Breaks always work. They just require a little extra effort if you're trying to have a blank page in there.

What I recommend, and you should do this anyway, is to be sure to check through your entire document when you're done and make sure that everything looks the way you want it. Okay.

Let's walk through this with an actual document that has headers and footers.

First, let's revisit the Headers & Footers Options section. As a reminder, you can add a header and/or footer to a document using the Header & Footer section of the Insert tab. When you do so, a Header & Footer tab will appear and in the Options section of that tab there will be three checkboxes:

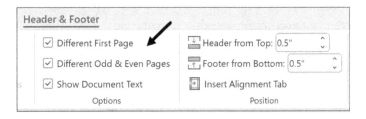

Different First Page is what you need to use when the first page of your document or your section should have a different header and/or footer than the other pages.

Different Odd & Even Pages is what allows you to have different text on the left-hand page and the right-hand page, like in a book where you have author name on one side and book title or chapter title on the other.

Here, I've set it up so that there is no header on the first page, consistent page numbering on the bottom of all pages, and then the even-numbered pages have an author name and the odd-numbered pages have a book title in the header.

To get this to work, I had to add the page numbering to the first page, first even-numbered page, and first odd-numbered page separately.

I zoomed my document to 50% so we can see six pages at once:

It may be hard to see, but the top of that first page is blank. On the next page, in the header we have the author name. On the next one after that, in the header we have the book title. And then you can see for the next three pages how those alternate in the header between author name and title. Each page where you can see the footer has a page number that goes up by one with each page.

Problem is, that second page is the start of a new chapter, so the header should be blank. Same with the fourth page and sixth page that we can see.

To fix this, each of those pages needs to be the start of a new section.

It is a best practice when adding section breaks to start on page 1 and then work your way through the document and add those breaks as you go. The reason to do this is because as you add breaks the page numbers will shift and that may impact what kind of break you use on later chapters.

Theoretically, if you're using odd-numbered or even-numbered page breaks it won't matter, but for me I prefer to assume I'll have issues and do what I can to avoid them up front.

So I start by going to page 1 and replacing that Page Break with an Odd Page Section Break.

(Be careful that when you replace a Page Break with a Section Break, that you replace it, not add to it. The first time I did this, I highlighted Page Break and then inserted the Section

Break and it kept the Page Break and inserted the Section Break before it. I had to delete the Page Break first and then add the Section Break to get it to work.)

You can see here that now my "second" page also does not have a header, which is what we wanted:

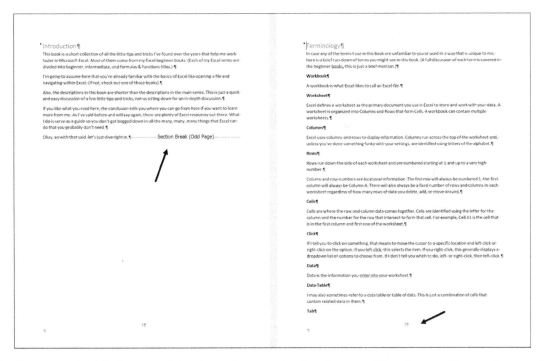

But I want to highlight something here that may be hard to see. That "second" page is actually the third page of the document. Because I used an Odd Page Section Break, Word, behind the scenes, has added a blank page between these two chapters. But it does not show on the screen. Nor does it show in Print Preview.

That blank page will only show up when the document is printed or generated as a PDF. You have to watch out for this because it is not intuitive to realize that there is a page that exists there but is not visible. Here is what that looks like when generated as a PDF:

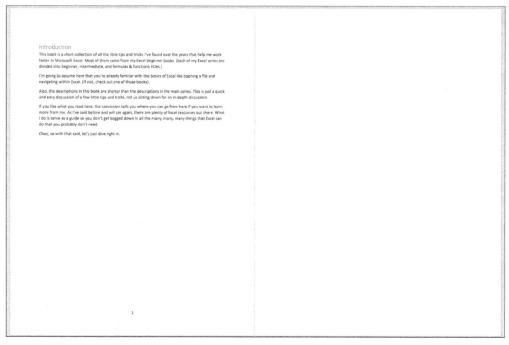

I can now walk through the rest of my document and replace my page breaks with section breaks. I want to have each chapter start on an odd-numbered page, so I will use the Odd Page Section Break.

Word carries through the header and footer settings from the original document, so each new chapter has a blank first page header and then uses the author name and book title on the even- and odd-numbered pages, respectively. Each page is also numbered at the bottom.

For this book here, as written, that would be the end of it. But let's change things up a bit. I combined a few of my chapters so I'd have enough pages in each chapter to see the book title at the top of the page. Here are six pages from the middle of the book across two "chapters":

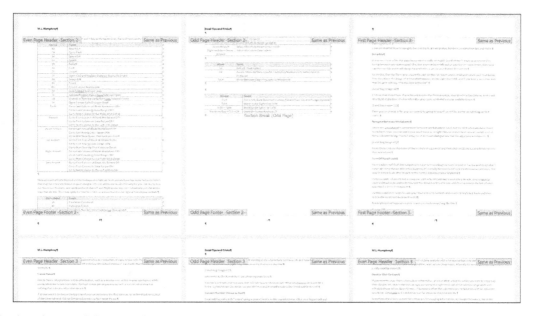

The headers and footers right now in these sections are linked. That means that any change I make to any of those headers or footers will carry over between the sections. For example, I just bolded the text in the headers for those first two pages and that bolding carried over to the bottom three pages.

But if you're trying to use different text at the top of a page for a section, you don't want that. The way to unlink your sections is to go to the Navigation section of the Header & Footer tab and unselect the Link to Previous option.

This is selected by default. Click into the second of the linked headers or footers first before you choose to unlink a header or footer since the option is to link to *previous*. Once you've unlinked your section from the prior section, you can edit the header or footer and it will not impact the prior section's header or footer.

If you are transitioning between front matter, like a table of contents, to the main body of your document or from the main body of your document to a standalone appendix, or using your chapter names for the header text, then you will need to do this.

I often find that I forget about this and make a change and then have to go back and unlink sections and then fix the one I inadvertently changed.

In my experience, working with section breaks and different headers and footers between those sections can take a little bit of trial and error to get everything to work properly. This is usually more about figuring out what should or should not be linked and making changes where they need to be made, but sometimes it seems to me that Word is more prone to do weird things the more complex your document becomes. So, don't get discouraged. Just fix things as they break and sometimes maybe find a simpler option (like a Next Page break instead of an Odd or Even Page break.)

Columns and Column Breaks

Since we just touched on it briefly above, I'm going to take a quick minute here and tell you how to change your document so that it has multiple columns of text on a single page.

First step, select your text that you want to place into multiple columns. Next, go to the Page Setup section of the Layout tab and click on the dropdown arrow below Columns.

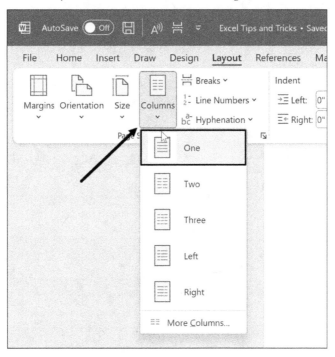

Choose your desired number of columns from the dropdown, which gives the option of one, two, or three columns as well as an option that has a skinnier left or right column next to a larger column.

If none of those options work for you, click on the More Columns option to bring up the Columns dialogue box:

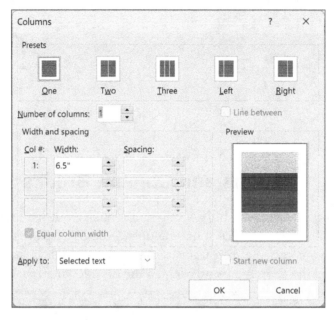

The dialogue box has those same options, but it also lets you specify different column widths for each column if you want.

You can also put a line between your columns if you want, like I've done here:

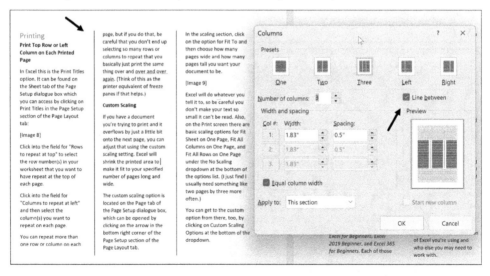

When you apply columns to a text selection, the default is for Word to spread that text evenly across the desired number of columns. Like so:

Workbook¶

A·workbook·is·what·Excel· likes·to·call·an·Excel·file.¶

Worksheet¶

Excel·defines·a·worksheet·as· the·primary·document·you· use·in·Excel·to·store·and· work·with·your·data.·A· worksheet·is·organized·into· Columns·and·Rows·that·form· Cells.·A·workbook·can· contain·multiple·worksheets.¶

Columns¶

Excel·uses·columns·and·rows· to·display·information.· Columns·run·across·the·top· of·the·worksheet·and,·unless· you've·done·something·funky· with·your·settings,·are· identified·using·letters·of·the· alphabet.¶

Rows¶

Rows·run·down·the·side·of· each·worksheet·and·are· numbered·starting·at·1·and· up·to·a·very·high·number.¶

Column·and·row·numbers· are·locational·information.·

The·first·row·will·always·be· numbered·1,·the·first·column· will·always·be·Column·A.· There·will·also·always·be·a· fixed·number·of·rows·and· columns·in·each·worksheet· regardless·of·how·many·rows· of·data·you·delete,·add,·or· move·around.¶

Cells¶

Cells·are·where·the·row·and· column·data·comes·together.· Cells·are·identified·using·the· letter·for·the·column·and·the· number·for·the·row·that· intersect·to·form·that·cell.· For·example,·Cell·A1·is·the· cell·that·is·in·the·first·column· and·first·row·of·the· worksheet.¶

Click¶

If·I·tell·you·to·click·on· something,·that·means·to· move·the·cursor·to·a·specific· location·and·left-click·or· right-click·on·the·option.·If· you·left-click,·this·selects·the· item.·If·you·right-click,·this· generally·displays·a· dropdown·list·of·options·to·

choose·from.·If·I·don't·tell· you·which·to·do,·left-·or· right-click,·then·left-click.¶

Data¶

Data·is·the·information·you· enter·into·your·worksheet.¶

Data·Table¶

I·may·also·sometimes·refer· to·a·data·table·or·table·of· data.·This·is·just·a· combination·of·cells·that· contain·related·data·in·them.¶

Tab¶

Tabs·are·the·options·you· have·to·choose·from·at·the· top·of·the·workspace.·The· default·tab·names·are·File,· Home,·Insert,·Page·Layout,· Formulas,·Data,·Review,· View,·and·Help.·But·there·are· certain·times·when· additional·tabs·will·appear,· for·example,·when·you· create·a·pivot·table·or·a· chart.¶

(This·should·not·be·confused· with·the·Tab·key·which·can· be·used·to·move·across· cells.)¶·Section Break (Continuous)·

Here I've taken a text selection and placed the text into three columns. If you read the entries, the text goes all the way down the first column and then continues to the second and then to the third. But because it's a selection, the amount of text in each column is about the same.

If you apply columns to an entire document instead, it will fill the first column on the page and then move on to the next column and then the next. In situations where there isn't enough text to fill the page you end up with something like this:

Printing

Print Top Row or Left Column on Each Printed Page

In Excel this is the Print Titles option. It can be found on the Sheet tab of the Page Setup dialogue box which you can access by clicking on Print Titles in the Page Setup section of the Page Layout tab.

[Image 8]

Click into the field for "Rows to repeat at top" to select the row number(s) in your worksheet that you want to have repeat at the top of each page.

Click into the field for "Columns to repeat at left" and then select the column(s) you want to repeat on each page.

You can repeat more than one row or column on each page, but if you do that, be careful that you don't end up selecting so many rows or columns to repeat that you basically just print the same thing over and over and over again. (Think of this as the printer equivalent of freeze panes if that helps.)

Custom Scaling

If you have a document you're trying to print and it overflows by just a little bit onto the next page, you can adjust that using the custom scaling setting. Excel will shrink the printed area to make it fit to your specified number of pages long and wide.

The custom scaling option is located on the Page tab of the Page Setup dialogue box, which can be opened by clicking on the arrow in the bottom right corner of the Page Setup section of the Page Layout tab.

In the scaling section, click on the option for Fit To and then choose how many pages wide and how many pages tall you want your document to be.

[Image 9]

Excel will do whatever you tell it to, so be careful you don't make your text so small it can't be read. Also, on the Print screen there are basic scaling options for Fit Sheet on One Page, Fit All Columns on One Page, and Fit All Rows on One Page under the No Scaling dropdown at the bottom of the options list. (I just find I usually need something like two pages by three more often.)

You can get to the custom option from there, too, by clicking on Custom Scaling Options at the bottom of the dropdown.

Conclusion

Okay. That was just a short set of quick tips and tricks that I use to make Excel easier and faster to work with, some of which I wish I'd known during my corporate career but have picked up while writing these books.

It is by no means a thorough introduction to any of the topics covered here. The Excel Essentials books when put together are an inch thick, so there is far, far more to Excel than this.

If you liked my way of explaining things and you want to learn more about Excel, then you may want to check one of those other books out.

The beginner titles, which most of this came from, are *Excel for Beginners*, *Excel 2019 Beginner*, and *Excel 365 for Beginners*. Each of these titles is designed to take you from absolute beginner through to about 95% of what you need to use Excel on a daily basis.

The intermediate titles, *Intermediate Excel*, *Excel 2019 Intermediate*, and *Intermediate Excel 365* explore more advanced topics like conditional formatting, pivot tables, and charts. So more data analysis.

And then the final titles are the formulas and functions titles. The original series had two of them, *50 Useful Excel Functions* and *50 More Excel Functions*. The later series have just one, *Excel 2019 Formulas & Functions* and *102 Useful Excel Functions*.

Which series is best for you will depend on which version of Excel you're using and who else you may need to work with.

If it's just you and you have Excel 2021 or Excel 365, then use the Excel 365 titles.

If you have Excel 2019 and aren't worried about working with anyone with an older version of Excel, then use the Excel 2019 books.

If you have an older version of Excel than 2019 or are working with people who have older versions of Excel, then the original Excel Essentials series is the one you want. That series was written to work for anyone in any version of Excel. It doesn't have the latest bells and whistles (like IFS or TEXTJOIN or XLOOKUP), but it also ensures that you can work with anyone in any version of Excel.

Okay. Hope this helped and you learned something you didn't know before. And hope maybe it prompted you to check out one of the other books, too.

See how on the left-hand page there are only two columns with text in them and how on the right-hand page there are only two lines of text in the last column but the other two columns are full?

To balance the text across a page, click at the very end of the text on that page and then apply a Continuous Section Break. (Page Setup section of the Layout tab, Breaks dropdown, Section Breaks, Continuous.) Your result will look something like this:

As mentioned above in the chapter on section breaks, if you add columns to a selection of text in your document, Word will automatically add the Continuous Section Breaks for you at the start and at the end of the selection.

Sometimes where the text falls naturally is not going to be what you want. Like here:

Workbook	Excel defines a worksheet as the primary document you use in Excel to store and work with your data. A worksheet is organized into Columns and Rows that form Cells. A workbook can contain multiple worksheets.
A workbook is what Excel likes to call an Excel file.	
Worksheet	

I put these entries into two columns, but the problem is that "Worksheet" naturally falls at the bottom of the left-hand column when it would be better placed at the top of the right-hand column.

You can force the text to break at a different point by inserting a Column Break. To do so, click where you need the break and then go to the Page Setup section of the Layout Tab and choose Column from the Breaks dropdown menu.

Much better:

Workbook	**Worksheet**
A workbook is what Excel likes to call an Excel file.	Excel defines a worksheet as the primary document you use in Excel to store and work with your data. A worksheet is organized into Columns and Rows that form Cells. A workbook can contain multiple worksheets.

Okay, so that was columns and column breaks. Now on to tables.

Tables

When I was in a corporate job we used tables all the time, so this is one that's definitely worth mastering. But if you really want to be good with tables you not only need to be able to insert them into a document, you need to format them properly, too, so this is going to be a long chapter.

Insert

To insert a table, go to the Insert tab and click on the dropdown for Table in the Tables section:

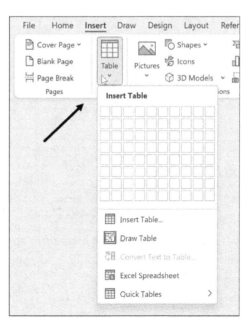

Under that Insert Table section, you can hold your mouse over the number of rows and columns you want in your table and Word will draw that for you in the document. Like so:

Click to insert the table.

Don't worry so much about the number of rows, but it is nice to start with the proper number of columns. (To add new rows to a table you can just go to the last cell in the table and use the Tab key and Word will add another row, so especially if you're directly entering the values in the table, the number of rows is easy to fix as needed.)

If you click on Insert Table in that dropdown instead, it will open the Insert Table dialogue box which lets you specify a number for columns and rows and also specify the AutoFit behavior for the table (fixed width, fit to contents, fit to window).

Another option is the Draw Table option, which is located in that same dropdown menu. It basically lets you left-click and drag to place a rectangle and then left-click and drag to draw lines within it, but I never use that option myself.

The Quick Tables option is another one I don't use. It inserts a pre-formatted table template.

The Excel Spreadsheet option will embed a working Excel spreadsheet into your document that displays as a table. When you're working in that one, your interface up top will actually be the Excel interface. But when you click away it will look like an ordinary table. Double-click on the table to get back into the Excel interface.

For working with calculations, the Excel Spreadsheet option is probably a better choice than trying to work directly in Word, but all of your formatting of that table will have to happen in the Excel interface, because once you close the interface Word will treat the table as a picture that can't be formatted or edited.

For this book we're just going to stick to a basic table.

When you insert a normal table in Word, you will see two new tabs appear at the top of the workspace, Table Design and Layout. There are a number of formatting choices you can make there, but first I just want to talk about a basic table using the Home tab options.

Here I've inserted a table in my document:

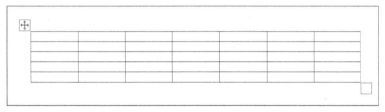

Now let's walk through how to add text and format that table.

Add Text

To input text into the table, you can click into a cell and type. Use the Tab key to move to the next cell in a row or Shift + Tab to move back one cell. If you're at the end of a row, it will move you to the next cell on the row below or above, depending on which direction you were moving.

If you have data to paste into your table, select all of the cells in the table first that will contain that data and then paste (Ctrl + V or one of the paste special options). If you don't select cells first, the data will all paste into that one cell where your cursor was. If you select less than the required number of cells, only the data for those cells will paste in. If you select too many cells, the data will paste in more than once to fill the selected number of cells.

Delete Text

To delete the text in a specific cell, select that text and then use the Backspace or Delete key. If you need to delete text in more than one cell at a time, use the Delete key.

If you select text in more than one cell or select an entire cell and try to use the Backspace key, Excel will want to also delete the cell not just the text. You'll see a Delete Cells dialogue box appear. You can close that box if that wasn't your intent, or choose one of the listed options if that was what you wanted to do.

Delete Contents of Table

To delete the contents of the entire table, click on the white box with four arrows in the top left corner of the table and then use the Delete key.

Delete Table

To delete the entire table, click on the white box with four arrows in the top left corner of the table and then use the Backspace key.

You can also use Cut once the table is selected or go to the Rows & Columns section of the table Layout tab, use the Delete dropdown menu, and choose Delete Table.

Format Text

You can format any text in a table just like you would other text. Select the cell(s) you want to format and then use the Font section of the Home tab or Ctrl shortcuts to apply your formatting. There are also alignment and text direction options in the Alignment section of the Layout tab.

Shading

One type of formatting that we didn't discuss in *Word 365 for Beginners* is Shading. That's because I usually only use it for tables. I like to have the first row of a table use a shaded background behind my text. Like so:

Value	Decimal Places	ROUND	ROUNDUP	ROUNDDOWN
3.124	2	3.12	3.13	3.12
3.126	2	3.13	3.13	3.12
-3.1246	2	-3.12	-3.13	-3.12
-3.1262	2	-3.13	-3.13	-3.12

That lets me distinguish my labels from my data.

To apply shading, select those cell(s), and then go to the Paragraph section of the Home tab. The Shading option is in the bottom row on the right-hand side. It looks like a paint bucket tilted to the right.

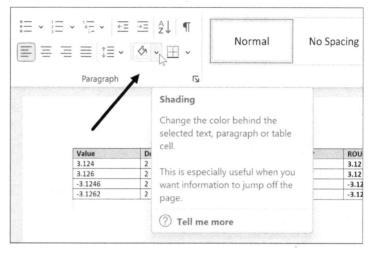

Click on the dropdown arrow to see the available color choices:

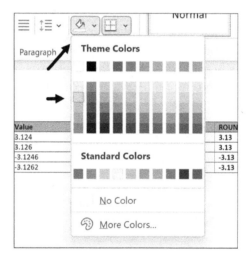

There are seventy colors there to choose from, but if you need a different color you can click on More Colors to open the Color dialogue box. The No Color option is what to use to remove shading from your selected cell(s).

There is also a Shading option in the Table Styles section of the Table Design tab as well as in the mini formatting menu.

Borders

By default, when you insert a table in Word it will have a border around all four sides of each cell. If you want to remove or edit the style of one of those borders, you can use the Borders dropdown in the Paragraph section of the Home tab:

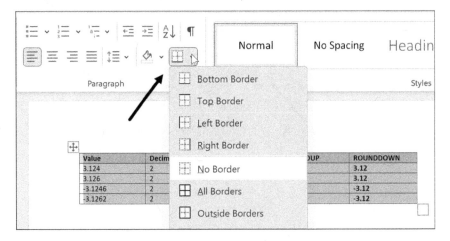

The borders that are currently applied to the table will be shaded in gray. The borders that are not currently in use will be unshaded. Hold your mouse over each option to see what the table will look like if that border is removed or added. Click to apply that change.

If you click on the Borders and Shading option at the bottom of the dropdown menu, that will open the Borders and Shading dialogue box which will let you change the line width, style, or color. Make those changes before applying new borders to your table.

Choose the Custom setting and use the Preview section to choose which lines to change if you want to use more than one line style, width, or color in your table at a time.

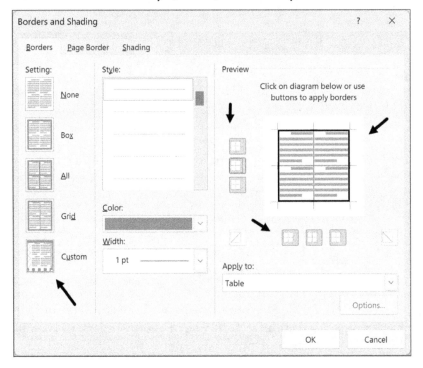

You can also select just a subset of the cells in the table to format those differently if needed, like I did here for the top row of this table which needed a different cell border than the main cells in the table:

Value	Decimal Places	ROUND	ROUNDUP	ROUNDDOWN
3.124	2	3.12	3.13	3.12
3.126	2	3.13	3.13	3.12
-3.1246	2	-3.12	-3.13	-3.12
-3.1262	2	-3.13	-3.13	-3.12

The Table Design tab also has a Borders section where you can choose your line style, line weight, and line color. If you make all of your selections there, you can then use the Border Painter and click on individual lines within your table to change their formatting:

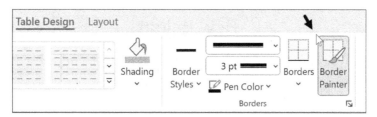

There is also a Borders dropdown menu there, but if you want to use it be sure to select the whole table or the cells you want to format first before making your selection.

You can also right-click on your table and choose Border Styles from the dropdown menu there to choose from a selection of twenty-one line styles which you can then apply one cell border at a time by clicking on the cell border.

Column Width

To manually adjust the width of a column in a table, left-click on the right-hand or left-hand border for that column and then hold that left-click and drag:

Value	Decimal Places	ROUND
3.124	2	3.12
3.126	2	3.13
-3.1246	2	-3.12
-3.1262	2	-3.13

(If you have your cursor positioned in the right spot it will turn into two vertical lines with arrows pointing in either direction.)

If you click and drag in the direction of another column, it will also change the width of the neighboring column so that the total width of the two columns combined remains the same. If you click and drag from the outer perimeter of the first or last column in the table, it will change the overall width of the table.

You can also right-click and choose to Distribute Columns Evenly or you can click on Distribute Columns in the Cell Size section of the Layout tab if you want all of your columns to be the same width.

Another option is to right-click on the column and choose Table Properties from the dropdown menu. Go to the Column tab and choose a new value for the Preferred Width of that column.

Or you can go to the table Layout tab and change the value for Width under Cell Size.

Both of those last two options will change the overall width of the table as well.

I will often combine the left-click and drag option on the first or last column to change the overall width of the table and then use that Distribute Columns option to fix the width of the columns based on the new table width.

Row Height

As you type text into a cell in Word the height of that row will automatically adjust so that all of the text is visible. (See image below for an example.) It is not possible to change a row height to hide any text in that row.

But you can left-click and drag along the upper or lower border of a cell to change the row height so that there's more space than the text takes up. (The cursor will look like two parallel lines with arrows pointing up and down when you have it positioned correctly.)

Value and then a lot of text to give this a new height	Decimal Places	ROUND	ROUNDUP	ROUNDDOWN
3.124	2	3.12	3.13	3.12
3.126	2	3.13	3.13	3.12
-3.1246	2	-3.12	-3.13	-3.12
-3.1262	2	-3.13	-3.13	-3.12

You can also open the Table Properties dialogue box or change the Height value in the Cell Size section of the table Layout tab.

If you choose Distribute Rows in the table Layout tab or Distribute Rows Evenly by right-clicking, that will resize your rows so that they are all the same size based upon the cell that is the tallest. Like here where all rows are now the height of the header row:

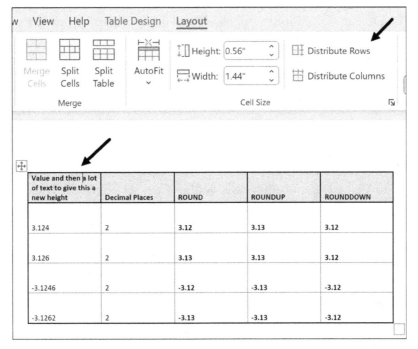

Space Between Cells or Around Table

To add space between cells or around the perimeter of your table, use the Cell Margins option in the Alignment section of the Layout tab to open the Table Options dialogue box.

Changing the value for Default Cell Spacing will add a space between the cells in each row and column. You can see that in the image below where each cell of the table is separated from the other cells in the table:

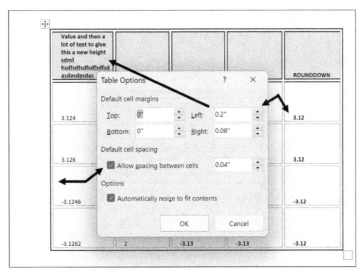

Adjusting the Default Cell Margins values adds space between the borders of each cell and the text within the cells.

You can see an example of this in the left-hand cell in the column header row where the text is indented from the left-hand side by .2" and from the right-hand side by only .08". Note how the text in that cell is visibly closer to the right-hand side of the cell.

Repeat Header Row

If you have a table that stretches across more than one page, then you will likely want to have the header row for that table on both pages. Rather than try to manually do that, which you should not do, there is an option that allows you to repeat the header row.

This is available in the Data section of the table Layout tab. Click on the option there.

Or you can right-click and choose Table Properties to open the Table Properties dialogue box and then go to the Row tab and check the box there.

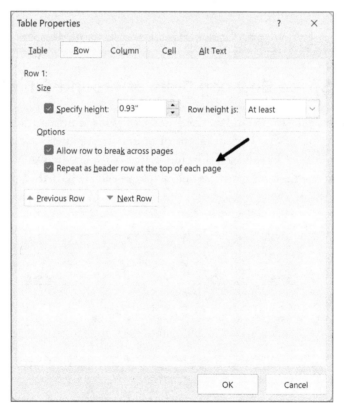

That option is only available for the first row of the table.

Insert Rows or Columns

We already discussed how to add an extra row to the end of a table. Just use Tab from the last cell in the table and Word will automatically add another row. But sometimes you will want to add a row(s) or column(s) in the midst of a table. Click on that location and then you have two options.

The first option is the Rows & Columns section of the table Layout tab:

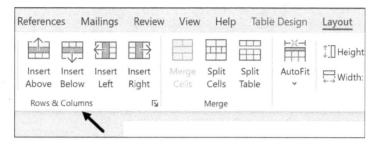

But I usually just right-click on the table and choose Insert from the dropdown menu and then my desired option from that secondary dropdown menu:

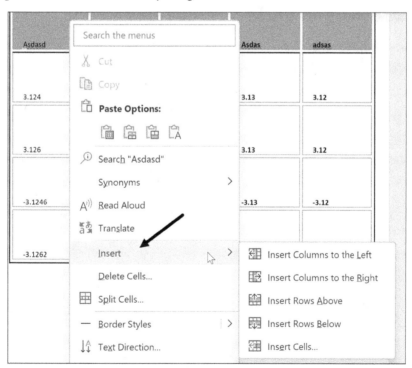

Note that if you insert columns that will change the overall width of your table so you may have to make adjustments after doing so to get the table to fit on the page again.

Delete Rows or Columns

To delete a column or row in a table, right-click on a cell in the column or row you want to delete and then choose the Delete option from the dropdown menu. This will bring up the Delete Cells dialogue box where you can choose to delete the entire row or column.

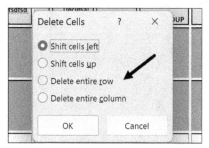

Your other option is to use the Delete dropdown menu in the Rows & Columns section of the Layout tab. Or to select one or more cells in that row or column and then use the Backspace key to bring up the Delete Cells dialogue box.

Delete Cell(s)

I don't recommend doing this, but it is possible to delete a single cell in a table using the above options.

Resize Table

To resize a table, right-click, choose Table Properties from the dropdown menu, and then go to the Table tab of the Table Properties dialogue box and change the value for Preferred Width. Click on OK. This will change your column widths, so you will probably have to adjust those afterward.

(The other option, mentioned above, is to resize a column at one end or the other of your table.)

Move Table

To move a table, left-click on the square with four arrows in the top left corner of the table and then drag.

Split Table

To split your table into two separate tables, click into the row that you want to be the first row in the second table and then go to the Merge section of the table Layout tab and click on Split Table.

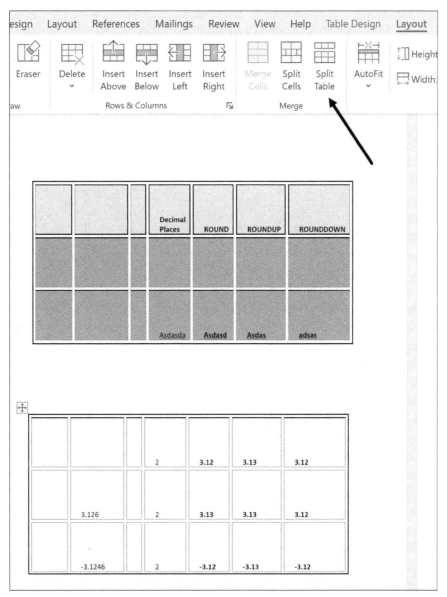

For whatever reason, when I just did this in my own document, it did split the tables but it placed them on top of one another, so I had to move one of the tables down to see both of them. (I don't recall it doing this in the past so I may have done something funky to cause that, but in case you do the same, that's how to fix it.)

Split Cells

You can split a cell in a table into multiple cells using the Split Cells option in the Merge section of the table Layout tab. Clicking on that option opens the Split Cells dialogue box which will let you specify a number of columns and rows for your split.

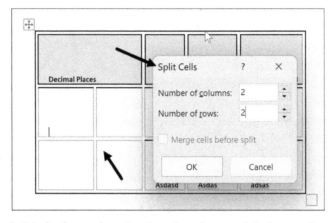

I believe I have used this before when I wanted to have a label row that covered more than one column, like Decimal Places now does above those two columns. But I may have also used Merge Cells for that instead.

This one is weird if there is already text in those cells. If you choose Merge Cells Before Split, it seems to bring that text up to the first X entries where X is the number of original cells in your selection. Otherwise, it puts the text in the left-most cell and doesn't let you split cells across rows. Best to do this before there's text involved.

Also, when you fill in the Split Cells dialogue box, the number of rows is the total number of rows for your selection, so if you selected two rows' worth of cells but then put 1 for the Number of Rows, that would actually merge those cells.

Merge Cells

To merge cells in a table, select the cells you want to merge and then use the Merge Cells option in the Merge section of the table Layout tab. It will automatically merge all of those cells and combine their contents into multiple rows of text within the cell.

Table Styles and Table Style Options

Finally, the Table Design tab has a number of Table Styles that are pre-formatted table style options:

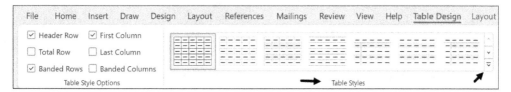

Click on the downpointing arrow with a line above it to see all of them:

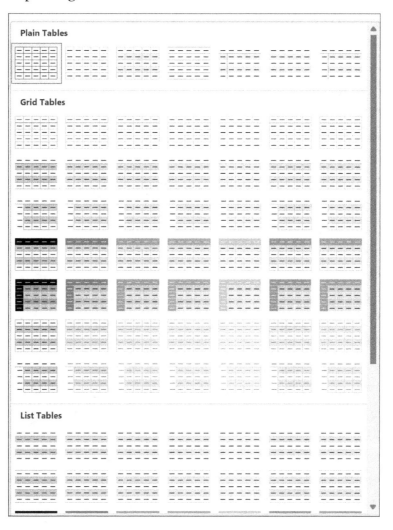

You'll have to use your scroll bar on the right-hand side to see the last few.

Click on any of those styles to apply it to your table. If you don't want to use the header row, first column, total row, last column, banded rows, or banded columns portion of the style, you can uncheck the box for that option in the Table Style Options section.

Or if you want to add that type of formatting, you can check those boxes.

As you check and uncheck those boxes the table styles will update to reflect how those changes will impact your table format. If the style has already been applied to your table, the table will also update.

I personally don't use table styles because they're never what I want so I just stick to a plain table style and then add my own shading as needed, but this is a way to get banded rows which can sometimes be useful. Just choose the Plain Table 1 option and uncheck Banded Columns if it's checked.

Symbols

To insert a symbol or character into your text, put your cursor where you want that symbol or character inserted and then go to the Symbols section of the Insert tab and click on the dropdown arrow. The dropdown will show twenty common symbols by default:

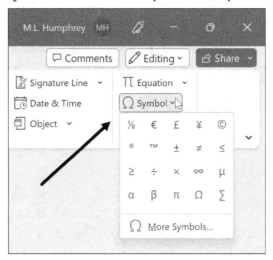

If you want one of those, click on it. (As you work in Word that list of symbols will change to reflect any symbols or characters you've used so that your most-recently-used symbols will be readily available to you.)

If you want a different character or symbol, then click on the More Symbols option to open the Symbol dialogue box.

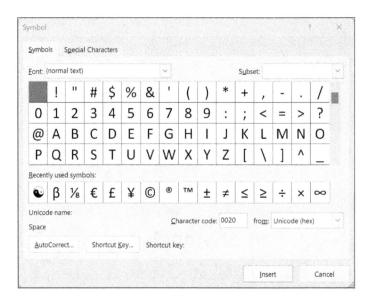

Sixteen common or recently-used symbols will display in a row towards the bottom of the dialogue box. But above that is a large area with sixty-four symbols visible. It has a scroll bar on the right-hand side that you can use to move through all available characters and symbols.

However, I usually like to use that Font dropdown that's located above the visible symbols to choose the font I want to use. The Wingdings fonts tend to have the most shapes available, for example:

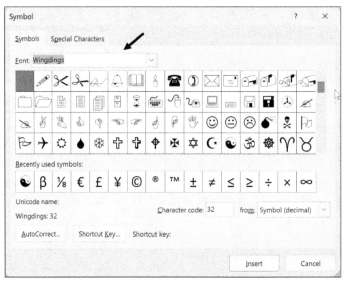

If you use a specific character or symbol often enough, you can create a keyboard shortcut for it by clicking on the Shortcut Key option at the bottom of the dialogue box and then assigning a shortcut using the Customize Keyboard dialogue box.

Many of the non-American-English letters already have shortcuts available that you can see in the bottom of the dialogue box when you select them:

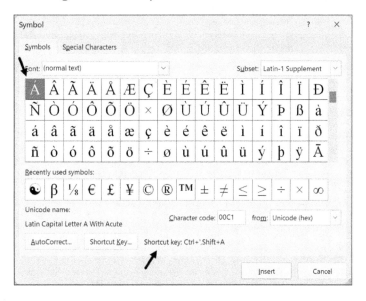

There is also a Special Characters tab that includes grammar marks and common symbols like the copyright and trademark symbols. Many of these also have keyboard shortcuts that are shown with them:

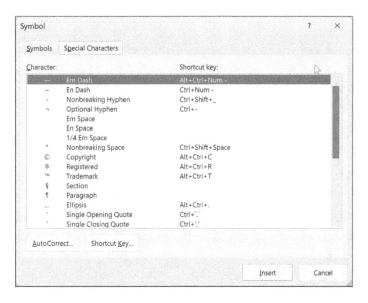

Some also have AutoCorrect options. If you click on that AutoCorrect button at the bottom, it will open the AutoCorrect dialogue box where you can see them:

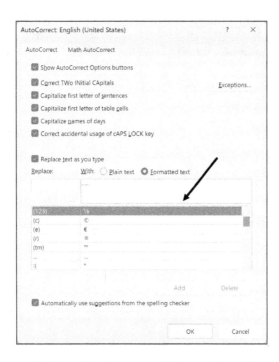

In this screenshot there are listings for the copyright, trademark, and registered symbols as well as the Euro symbol.

Once a symbol or character has been inserted into your document, it's treated like text. You can delete it just like you would any other text and also apply font size, color, bold, etc.

For special characters, as you change the font, the character may also change to match that font. For example, the copyright symbol looks different in different fonts. But shapes, like ones from the Wingdings fonts, will remain unchanged.

Here I've inserted five shapes or characters and then applied four different fonts to them:

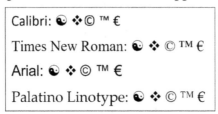

You can see that the first two Wingdings shapes remain unchanged, but that the C in the copyright symbol changes as does the TM in the trademark symbol. And that the Euro symbol is different between all four.

Which is a reminder, too, that if you copy a symbol from another document, be sure to paste it in with the Keep Text Only option so that it uses the font of your document.

Okay, that was symbols, now I want to touch very briefly on all the other things you can insert into a document.

Pictures and Shapes

In the Illustrations section of the Insert tab there are seven types of illustrations you can insert into your document: Pictures, Shapes, Icons, 3D Models, SmartArt, Chart, and Screenshot.

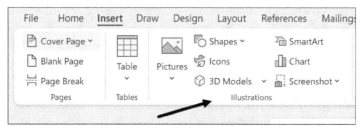

In this chapter we'll cover two of the most popular of those options, Pictures and Shapes.

Pictures

The Pictures option lets you insert a picture into your document.

The picture can either be one you have stored on your computer (or an external device like a thumb drive) or it can be one that comes from online pictures or stock images. If you want to insert a picture from OneDrive, use the Online Pictures option and change the dropdown from Bing to OneDrive.

If you use online pictures or stock images, be sure that you have the right to do so. It can be very costly to use an image you don't have the rights to and it's best to get into the habit of only using images that you either took yourself or have paid to use.

Here we're just going to walk through how to use the first option in the Pictures dropdown menu, Insert Picture From This Device.

When you choose that option, an Insert Picture dialogue box will appear that allows you to locate an image to insert. Navigate to where you have the image stored, click on it, and then click on Insert.

When you do so, the image will come into your document at a default size related to its overall properties and the size of your document.

A Picture Format tab will appear that lets you change the color settings, apply borders, change the image size, and adjust how the picture is positioned relative to your text or other objects:

To change the size of a picture, I recommend using the Size section of the Picture Format tab. By default the aspect ratio for your picture should be locked which means that if you change width or height it will adjust the other measurement as well to keep the image proportionate.

There are also white circles around the perimeter of an inserted image that you can left-click on and drag to resize an image, but be careful with pictures because if you do so from one of the sides, you can distort the image.

To delete an image, select it and then use the Delete or Backspace key.

Shapes

The Shapes option allows you to insert a variety of shapes into your document.

Click on the dropdown arrow next to Shapes to choose the shape you want. Here is the top part of that dropdown menu, but there are many more options.

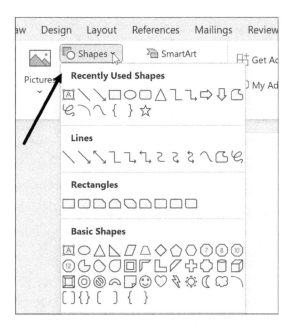

Click on the shape you want and then left-click and drag to insert the shape into your workspace.

When you create a shape there will be a Shape Format dialogue box that allows you to control color, size, and position relative to other objects and text in your document.

You can also make changes directly to the shape. Left-click on the white circles around the perimeter of a shape and then drag to change the size of the shape. Left-click on the yellow circles (when available) to change the shape itself. The little circle with an arrow at the top (when available) will allow you to rotate the shape.

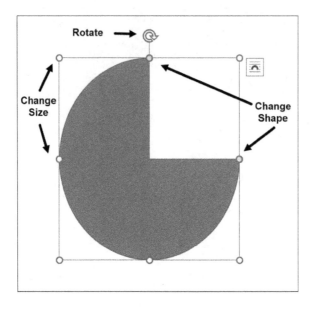

Click away from the shape to return to your text or other objects.

Formatting and Placement

As mentioned above, there will be a special Format tab that appears when you insert a Picture or Shape. The Styles menu has pre-formatted appearance settings and then to the right of that are more specific effects and formatting options.

The Position dropdown allows you to specify how the picture or shape should sit relative to your text.

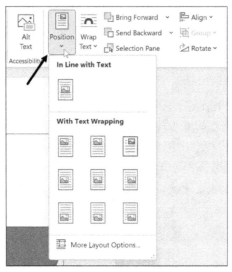

Each option has a visual representation that shows how the object will be positioned relative to your text. Click on More Layout Options to have more control over your object placement and how that object moves or relates to your text.

The Wrap Text dropdown specifies how text will interact with the object and, again, each choice has a small image that visually represents how that would look:

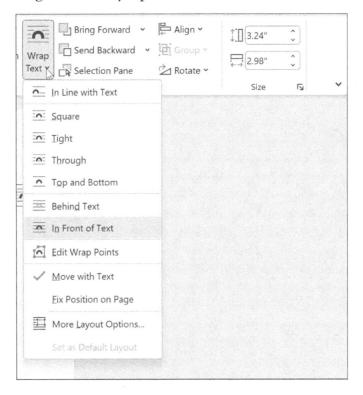

The other options in the Arrange section of each Format tab allow you to specify how different objects will interact with one another. You can specify which will be visible when two objects overlap or choose how to align objects either to one another or to the page.

Other Illustrations and Equations (Brief)

Now let us cover the remaining illustration types very briefly as well as equations.

Other Illustrations

The other options in the Illustrations section of the Insert tab are Icons, 3D Models, SmartArt, Chart, and Screenshot. They work much like Pictures or Shapes in the sense that you choose the one you want and insert it and then can use a Format tab to change attributes.

Icons

Icons require an internet connection before you can insert them in Word 365. They are stock images that are black line drawings of a variety of items like sunglasses, alarm clocks, apples, etc. When you click on this option you also have the ability to choose Cutout People, Stickers, Illustrations, and Cartoon People.

3D Models

3D Models are 3D images that you can insert into your document, some of which are animated. You can use the circle with rotating lines in the middle of the model when inserted to rotate up, down, or to the side.

SmartArt

SmartArt are various illustrative graphics that you can insert into Word that demonstrate processes, cycles, hierarchies, relationships, etc. You choose the graphic that you want to use and then can add your own values to that graphic.

When you insert one into your document a Type Your Text Here dialogue box should appear that lets you input those values. If you close the dialogue box the Text Pane option in the Create Graphic section of the SmartArt Design tab will bring it back up.

I discuss this more in the PowerPoint books, but just be careful when choosing SmartArt that the visual representation actually matches your values. I once saw someone, for example, using a pyramid SmartArt object for unrelated data. Don't do that. Your chosen visual should support the data not contradict it.

Chart

The Chart option will allow you to choose a type of chart to insert into your document. When you do so, there will be an Excel data table that appears on the screen where you can add the values that will build the chart. If you close that window and need to edit those values, use the Edit Data dropdown in the Chart Design tab to bring it back.

Screenshot

The screenshot option lets you take a screenshot of any of the other programs you have open on your computer. If you use the Screen Clipping option you can click and drag to select a subset of that image.

Equations

Directly above the Symbols option in the Symbols section of the Insert tab is an option for Equation that has a dropdown menu available:

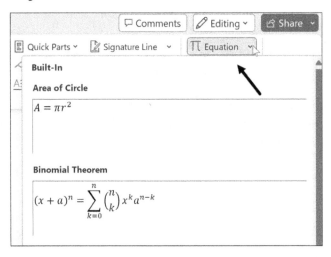

If you click on one of the listed equations, Word will insert that equation as shown into your document in a separate input box like it did here for Area of Circle:

You can choose a format for the equation that is either Professional or Linear. The image above uses a professional format where there is a superscript used for the 2. In linear that would show as ^2 instead and everything would be on one line.

Click on the dots on the left-hand side of that input box and drag to reposition the equation in your document.

If you want to create a custom equation, click on Equation in the Insert tab instead of using the dropdown menu. That will insert a blank box that says Type Equation Here and then you can use the Symbols and Structures sections of the Equation tab to build your equation:

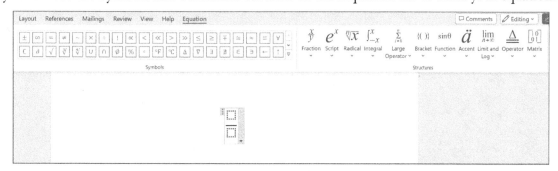

Above, I chose one of the options from the Fractions dropdown under the Structures section. I can now click on each of those dotted boxes and add numbers or symbols to build out the equation.

To delete an equation, select it by clicking on the dots on the left-hand side and then use the Backspace key. You can also use Cut to remove it once it's been selected.

MultiLevel Lists

Time for one of the most annoying topics I wanted to cover in this book, multilevel lists.

Why are they so annoying? If you use them as-is and for the entire document, they're not. But if you try to customize them it can be very painful. Same with if you try to use them in addition to other lists in the same document.

Also, last I checked, they need customization because they don't follow a standard format. The one I'm going to show you here, for example, is fine for the first three levels, but then uses an a with a paren instead of an a with a period, which is not how I was taught it should go.

But let's go look, shall we.

Multilevel lists can be found in the Paragraph section of the Home tab in the top row next to bulleted lists and numbered lists which were already covered in *Word 365 for Beginners*:

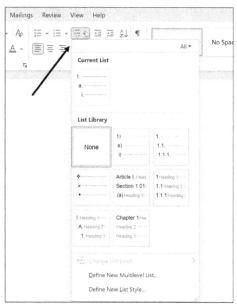

The list choice that's closest to what I was raised with in school is that third one down on the left in the list library, so I'm going to select it and then create a few entries.

Here's what I came up with:

> I.   This is the main level entry for this <u>topic</u>
> This is me adding text below that point.
>
> A.   Now I want a sub-entry.
> B.   And another sub-entry.
>   ◢ 1.   And a subpoint of that one.

A few points to mention here that are important.

With a bulleted or numbered list, when you hit Enter the next line is automatically also bulleted or numbered. With a multilevel list, that is not the case. The next line is text.

Furthermore, that text is not indented. The cursor goes back each time to the far left-hand side of the page.

Using the Tab key will get you to a point directly below the text in the prior line so you can add a description or paragraph like I did above under the first main point.

For those other entries, the A, the B, and the 1, I had to go up to the Paragraph section of the Home tab, click on the dropdown for Multilevel List, and then click on the current list I was using.

If your cursor is not already indented to the level you want, place the cursor before the text in that line and use the Tab key to move the text one indent level at a time.

Another option for getting the right list level is to go back to that dropdown and use the Change List Level option to choose the desired list level.

You can also use the Indent options in the Paragraph section of the Home tab.

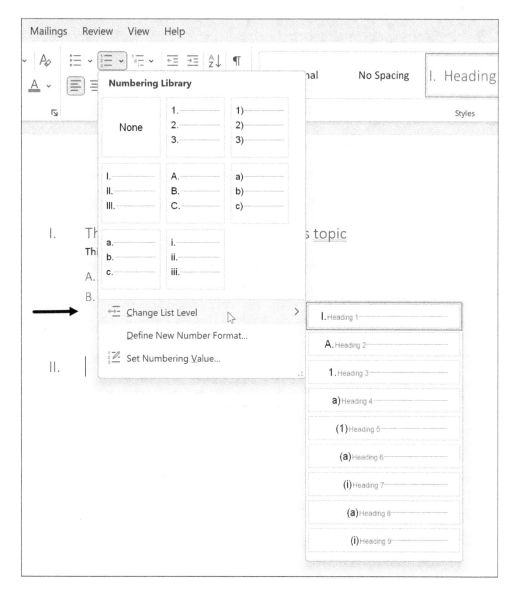

Each list level will have a black arrow that will appear to the left of the entry when you hold your mouse over it that you can click on to hide everything below that entry.

The nice thing about the multilevel list is that it does continue throughout your document even if there is text in between. So if I type text and then add a new multilevel list entry after that text, it will continue the numbering from above:

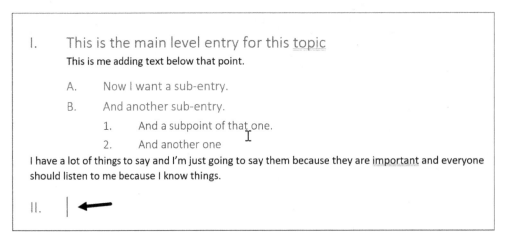

If the default numbering options don't work for you, you can choose Define New Multilevel List from the multilevel list dropdown to create your own list. That will open the Define New Multilevel List dialogue box where you can then for each level choose the number formatting to use, the alignment for the number, and the amount the text should be indented.

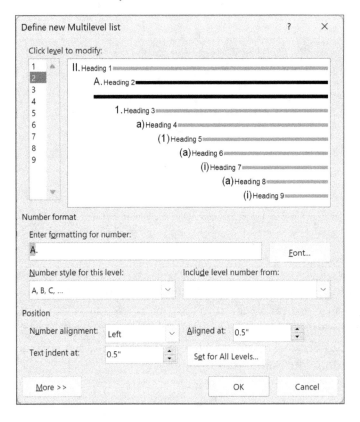

Click on More to see more options such as how to separate the number from the text (default is a Tab character) and where to apply those changes and what numbering to start at and when to restart that level's numbering.

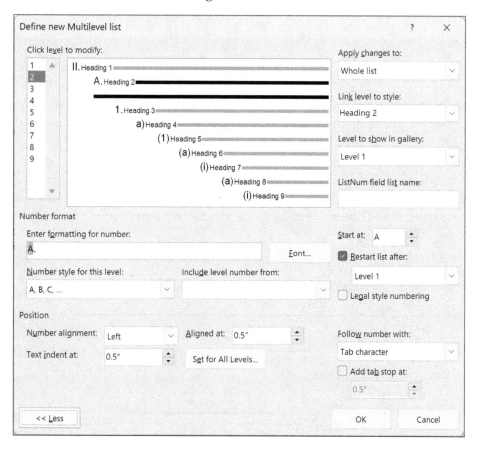

These list entries are tied into the Heading 1, Heading 2, etc. styles, which can be problematic. When I tried to add an entry using a multilevel list to the very end of an existing document that was already using Heading 1 for the chapter headers, Word automatically converted all of my prior chapter headers to parts of the multilevel list I'd just added.

You can see here that Heading 1 and Heading 2 now are formatted to be part of a multilevel list.

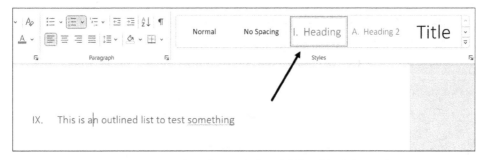

Which, hey if you're using that outline format for your entire document, is probably great, because it lets you quickly apply the multilevel list styles as needed as you write your document.

But if you were doing what I just tried to do, which is use a multilevel list at the end of the document, it's a disaster.

You can go back to that Define New Multilevel List option and change the setting that links the first level of the list to the Heading 1 style and click OK to fix that. But you need to do it for all of the levels. Here I fixed Heading 1, but you can see that Heading 2 is still tied into the multilevel list:

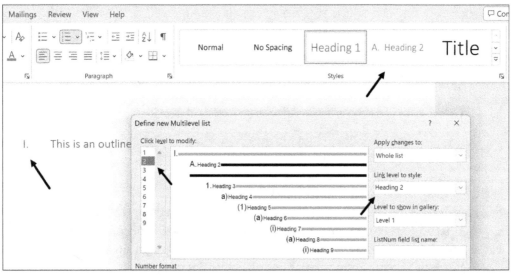

My advice to you if you want to use the multilevel list option is to make sure that your entire document uses the list and that there are no other Heading styles or other numbered or bulleted lists in the document.

Also, if you are trying to fix a document that has a multilevel list that isn't working properly, you may have to create that multilevel list in a new document and then paste in your text one paragraph at a time to fix it. (Hopefully not, but that is what I have had to do once or twice when nothing else would work.)

Not the best use of time, but it may be the only way to get it all to work the way it should.

Table of Contents

If you use styles, then you can have Word create a table of contents for you. To do that, assign Heading 1, Heading 2, etc. styles to the entries in your document that you want to include in the table of contents.

Next, go to the location in your document where you want to place the table of contents and go to the References tab. On the left-hand side is a dropdown menu for Table of Contents:

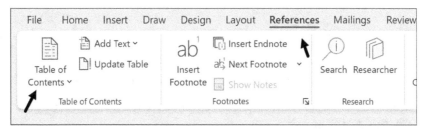

There are two pre-formatted table of content options you can choose and one manual table of contents option as well. The only difference between the two automatic tables of contents is whether it says Contents or Table of Contents. (The manual table of contents basically gives you formatting, but nothing else, so I'm not going to cover that one further.)

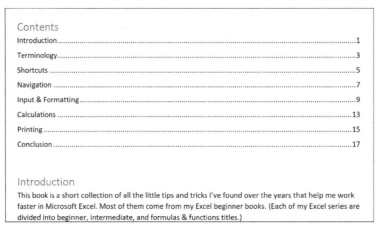

Built-In

Automatic Table 1

Contents
Heading 1...1
Heading 2...1
Heading 3 1

Automatic Table 2

Table of Contents
Heading 1...1
Heading 2...1
Heading 3 1

Manual Table

Table of Contents
Type chapter title (level 1)...1
Type chapter title (level 2)...2
Type chapter title (level 3)...3
Type chapter title (level 1)...4
Type chapter title (level 2)...5

🌐 More Tables of Contents from Office.com   >

📄 Custom Table of Contents...

📄 Remove Table of Contents

📄 Save Selection to Table of Contents Gallery...

You can also use the More Tables of Contents From Office.com option or you can choose to create a Custom Table of Contents.

I'm going to choose that first option there. And here we go:

Contents

Introduction
This book is a short collection of all the little tips and tricks I've found over the years that help me work faster in Microsoft Excel. Most of them come from my Excel beginner books. (Each of my Excel series are divided into beginner, intermediate, and formulas & functions titles.)

A few comments here. First, note that my first chapter is currently starting on the same page as my table of contents. To fix that I'd need to insert a page break. Also, I only had Heading 1 in use in this document, so I only have one level of table of contents entries for it to use.

If I go and apply Heading 2 to my sub-sections of my chapters, it doesn't automatically update. But I can right-click on the table and an Update Table option will appear at the top of the table. When I click on that I can then choose to update page numbers or the entire table in the Update Table of Contents dialogue box:

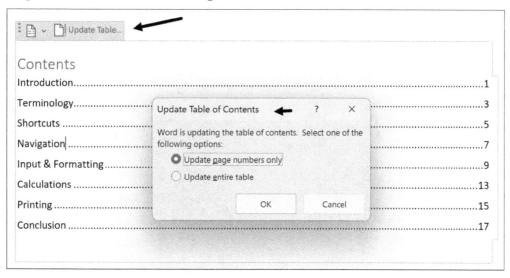

And here is my updated table of contents using Heading 1 and Heading 2:

Contents

Introduction..1

Terminology..3

    Workbook...3

    Worksheet..3

    Columns..3

    Rows..3

Shortcuts...5

Navigation...7

Input & Formatting...9

Calculations...13

Printing..15

Conclusion...17

Once you have a table of contents in your document, you can click on it and then use those three dots on the far left-hand side to left-click and drag your table of contents to a new location.

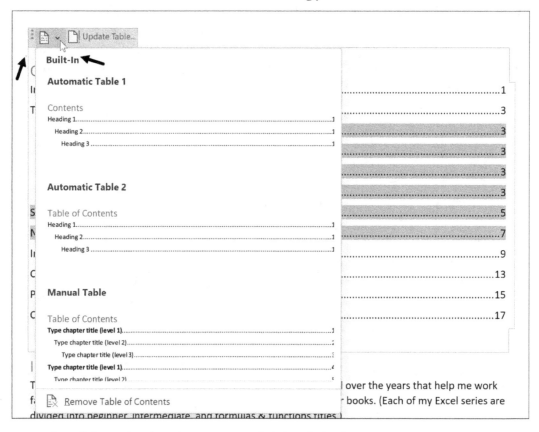

You can also click on the dropdown arrows for that little document next to the dots to bring up a dropdown menu. The bottom option in the dropdown lets you remove your table of contents.

It also displays the other default table of contents styles. You can move back and forth between Automatic Table 1 and Automatic Table 2 (just the title changes).

You can select your table of contents just like any other text in your document and change the font, but if you then update that table of contents it will revert to whatever font is being used for the entries that feed into the table.

Once there is an automatic table of contents in your document, you can use Ctrl and click on any of the entries in the table to go to that page in your document.

So what if those default styles aren't what you want? Let's go explore the Custom Table of Contents option now. Selecting that option brings up the Table of Contents dialogue box:

You can choose here whether or not to show page numbers, whether or not to right align those page numbers, what type of separator to use between the table of contents entries and the page numbers (dotted line, straight line, nothing), how many Heading levels to use to build the table of contents, and whether to use hyperlinks for the entries.

That Formats dropdown also lets you choose a variety of pre-formatted appearances that you can use for your table format.

Here for example I used a Modern Format and removed page numbers and hyperlinks:

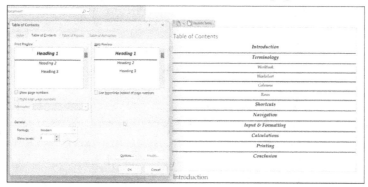

When I clicked on OK it asked if I wanted to replace my existing table of contents, so that's how to apply a new custom format to an existing table.

Unfortunately, reverting back to one of the two default automatic tables required me to delete the table of contents in my document, close it, and then re-open and insert a new table of contents. Otherwise I kept getting my custom format and would've had to manually change it back. (That could be a me issue not the program, but a workaround if you need it.)

If you want to use styles other than the Headings styles to populate your table of contents, click on Options in the Table of Contents dialogue box to bring up the Table of Contents Options dialogue box:

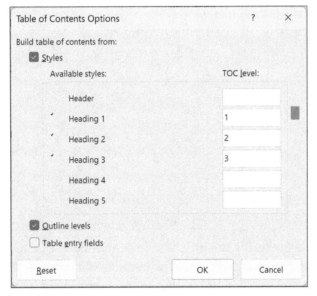

As you can see above, by default Heading 1 is the 1st level of the table of contents, Heading 2 is the 2nd level, and Heading 3 is the 3rd level, but all available styles are listed here, including any custom styles you used.

So I could remove 1 from the box for Heading 1 and put that value next to my custom style instead and then Word would use any entries with my custom style as the first level of my table of contents.

One last note, if you didn't use Headings as you created your document, you can use the Add Text option in the Table of Contents section of the References tab to assign text to the various table of content levels.

Select the text and then click on Add Text in the Table of Contents section of the References tab and choose the table of contents level you want for that text.

Word will assign that text the style that is being used for that level of your table of contents. So by default Level 1 will assign the style Heading 1. Which means you need to be careful if you don't want to change the formatting for that selected text.

Easier in my opinion to assign your styles as you work on your document, but an option if you need it.

Track Changes

Now we are up to track changes, which are amazing and wonderful and made my corporate life much, much easier.

When I first started we had a few people in my office who would manually format text to show changes. Which meant that you had to manually reformat that text to finalize the document. It was a nightmare.

With track changes, someone can make edits to your document and you can see those edits but then all you have to do is accept or reject those changes and they're incorporated into your document and you're done. It's fantastic.

Also, you can navigate through your document one change at a time so that you don't miss anything. No stray comma or period that gets skipped over because it's such a small change.

But you have to be careful with track changes. Some of the views that Word now offers with respect to track changes don't show them. So you can miss that there are track changes in a document and send it off to an outside party and they open it up and they see all of those little changes and who made them. Not a good thing.

If you use track changes, you have to be careful to accept all changes and turn them off when you're done.

Okay. Let's tackle this topic. I'm going to save comments, which go hand-in-hand with track changes, for the next chapter.

When you open a document that has track changes turned on, Word will now (as of January 2023 in Word 365) give you a warning message that track changes are on:

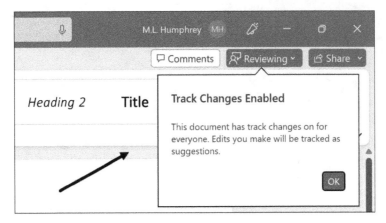

This is a good thing. You never want to work in a document that has track changes turned on without realizing you are doing so.

First things first.

Turn On or Off Track Changes

To turn on or off track changes you can use Ctrl + Shift + E. There is also an option to do so in the Tracking section of the Review tab:

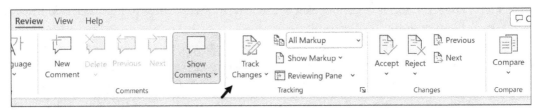

To turn on track changes, just click on that image that says Track Changes. To turn it off, click on it again. You want to click onto the image part of that option, not the text part. And you don't need the dropdown. So aim for the pen or pencil or whatever that is.

And I want to make a point here. It is possible to have a document that shows track changes, but that also has other changes that were made to the document that are not visible because someone temporarily turned off track changes and then made edits. So if it is really, really important that you see every single change in a document, use Document Compare to see all edits instead of trusting that track changes captured everything.

(Usually this is not some nefarious deliberate thing that happens. In past versions of Word I would turn off track changes when making formatting or non-essential changes to tables because the way Word showed track changes for tables was ugly and confusing and didn't really let people see what it would look like when final and most users don't want to see every little formatting change. But sometimes I'd also forget to turn it back on.)

Okay. So. Turn on track changes and make your edits.

Appearance

Here is an example of track changes with two different users:

> This is a sample document that I'm creating on my other computer to see if I can show you track changes made by ~~two~~ different users. It may or may not work because both of these computers are tied into the same Microsoft account. But let's give it a go.
>
> I have now turned T~~t~~rack ~~e~~Changes on in my document and you can see that any new text I add is underlined and colored a different color.
>
> This is me working on this same document on a different computer. I stripped out the Author information before I saved this version of this document so that I could appear as two different users.

Text additions that are recorded by Track Changes are underlined and color-coded. Deletions have a strikethrough and are also color-coded but are not underlined.

Above you can see that "two" in that first paragraph was deleted. And that the second and third paragraphs were all text that was added after Track Changes was turned on. The second paragraph is blue, the third is red, to indicate different users.

(For those of you reading in black and white, you won't be able to see the colors that distinguish the different users, but should still be able to see the additions and deletions.)

Also, you can see that in the second paragraph the first user wrote "track changes" and the second user changed that to "Track Changes".

For each tracked change, on the left-hand side of the text there is a vertical black line indicating that a change was made at that location.

Word automatically assigns colors to users and this can change, so you can't assume that a user will always be assigned the same color each time. The color assigned to a specific user will always be consistent within a document while that document remains open, but the color assigned to a user can change when the document is reopened

For example, when I wrote that first paragraph on my old laptop the changes were in red. But when I opened that document on my new laptop the changes were in blue. So you need to check each time when you review a document which user is assigned to which color.

Users

All changes made when Track Changes are turned on are assigned to users. By default, each user is assigned their own color. This is normally based upon the associated Microsoft Office account of the user, not the computer.

So, for example, when I worked on a document on one computer and then transferred it to another, my changes on the new computer were given the same color because both computers are tied into my Microsoft Office account. (I was able to get the two colors you can see in the example above only when I stripped the author information from the document after I made the first set of edits.)

To see who the user is for a specific edit, you have a couple options.

The first option is to hold your mouse over the edit:

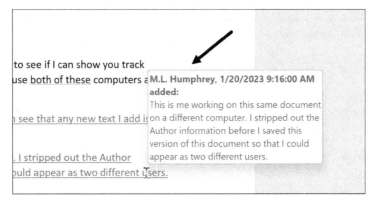

Note that also shows the time and date when the edit was made.

The second option is to show the Reviewing Pane.

Reviewing Pane

The Reviewing Pane can be turned on or off using the Reviewing Pane dropdown menu in the Tracking section of the Review tab:

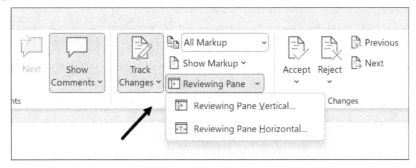

You have the choice of a vertical pane or a horizontal pane. My preference is for the vertical pane, although usually I don't actually use a reviewing pane at all:

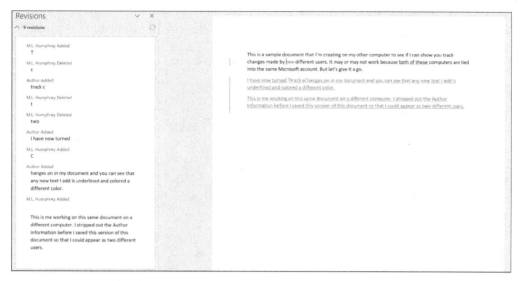

The Reviewing Pane will list each revision in the document as well as who made that revision. So you can see here that the two users that Word is tracking are Author and M.L. Humphrey.

The reason I'm not a huge fan of using it for simple track changes is because it's much easier for me to see what's happening in the document itself than to interpret that list of revisions.

For example, here:

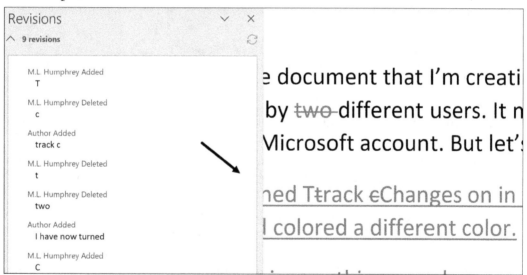

It's pretty easy looking at the text to see that one user wrote the words "track changes" and that another user came along and capitalized them so that it became "Track Changes".

But if I look in the Revisions panel, I have listings that tell me M.L. Humphrey added "T" and deleted "c" and that Author added "track c" and that M.L. Humphrey deleted "t" and then it lists two unrelated edits and finally tells me that M.L. Humphrey added "C".

The list of revisions is accurate, but reading through those edits one at a time is confusing. So I don't do it usually.

Track Changes Views

I personally like this view that's the default view for my track changes, All Markup. It shows me the old text as well as all edits that have been made. This is the view I try to keep active at all times unless I need a different view. But let's walk through those other choices in case you need them.

Simple Markup

This is the Simple Markup view:

> This is a sample document that I'm creating on my other computer to see if I can show you track changes made by different users. It may or may not work because both of these computers are tied into the same Microsoft account. But let's give it a go.
>
> I have now turned Track Changes on in my document and you can see that any new text I add is underlined and colored a different color.
>
> This is me working on this same document on a different computer. I stripped out the Author information before I saved this version of this document so that I could appear as two different users.

It has a red vertical line off to the side to indicate where edits have been made, but, other than that, it's the final document with all changes made.

It's good for seeing what the final product will look like. So a good last-pass option. It makes sure that you catch any extra spaces or double periods or things like that that can slip through when track changes are on.

But for me it is not a good working option. Many times I found as I was working with teams on projects that I really did need to know what was originally written, how that was changed, and who made the change. Hate to say it, but if the lawyer with twenty years of experience made the edit to that technical paragraph that was written by the brand new analyst I'm more likely to trust that edit was correct than if the brand new analyst edited something written by the lawyer. Context often matters.

No Markup

This is the No Markup view:

> This is a sample document that I'm creating on my other computer to see if I can show you track changes made by different users. It may or may not work because both of these computers are tied into the same Microsoft account. But let's give it a go.
>
> I have now turned Track Changes on in my document and you can see that any new text I add is underlined and colored a different color.
>
> This is me working on this same document on a different computer. I stripped out the Author information before I saved this version of this document so that I could appear as two different users.

It has no indication that there are any track changes in the document. The text reflects all of the changes that were made. But there is no way to see that track changes is on.

I would use this one only if I were printing off a copy of the document for review by a senior person who needed to review the "final" but where I wasn't yet willing to remove tracked changes yet. It would allow printing of a completely clean copy and wouldn't distract that senior person with notations of where changes had been made.

But I'd immediately get away from this view as soon as I printed the document. I would never leave a document in this view.

(As someone whose job used to be investigating financial institutions for rule violations that sometimes carried hefty fines, trust me that you don't want to forget that a document has track changes still visible.)

Original

This is the Original view:

> This is a sample document that I'm creating on my other computer to see if I can show you track changes made by two different users. It may or may not work because both of these computers are tied into the same Microsoft account. But let's give it a go.

This is another one I would never, ever leave my document in for any length of time. But sometimes it can be helpful to look at the document as it existed prior to any edits. Especially when there are multiple users making edits to the same text. That lets you see what the source text really was.

All Markup

And then finally, as a reminder, this is the All Markup view:

> This is a sample document that I'm creating on my other computer to see if I can show you track changes made by two different users. It may or may not work because both of these computers are tied into the same Microsoft account. But let's give it a go.
>
> I have now turned Ttrack eChanges on in my document and you can see that any new text I add is underlined and colored a different color.
>
> This is me working on this same document on a different computer. I stripped out the Author information before I saved this version of this document so that I could appear as two different users.

It shows the original text in black and then marks the location of any changes with a black vertical line off to the side of the text. All additions and deletions in the document are shown with colored text. For me, this is the best one to see what was done to the original text and whether I agree.

A Quick Warning

If it matters to you who made what changes in your document, then never ever do what I did above to give you these examples. I achieved that effect by stripping out the Author information from the document. And right now that All Markup example looks great. It has changes by two distinct users and we can see what each of them did. But as soon as I save changes to that document, all of the changes will be assigned to Author.

I had this happen on a big project. Some analyst stripped out the author information from the original document and then circulated it to a team of six for edits. And no one noticed what was happening until we had a final document where all edits appeared as if they'd been made by one user. It was horrible.

So if you must strip out the author information from a document, save a copy of that document as it existed right before you do that and then strip those properties out of your document only when the document is final and ready to be distributed. Never strip author information from a document that is still a work in progress that may require the use of track changes.

Show Markup Options

One final basic appearance setting that we have not yet covered is the Show Markup dropdown menu available in the Tracking section of the Review tab:

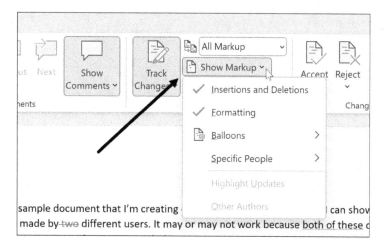

By default, Word will show both insertions/deletions and formatting changes. Here is an example with formatting changes included:

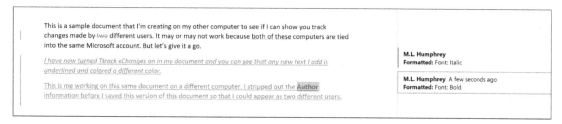

There are times when you really don't need to see all the formatting changes. I am a control freak so I always wanted to see them, but for a lawyer whose focus is on the words and the commas, they don't need to see that you reformatted the headers throughout the document.

So if you don't want to see the formatting changes listed out, click on that option to turn it off. Or if you do want to see them and they're off, click on that option to turn it on.

You can also choose how changes in the document are shown. By default, only formatting changes are shown in "balloons" which are the notes off to the side, but you can actually choose to show all revisions that way or to show all revisions inline in the document:

Here is an example that shows revisions in balloons:

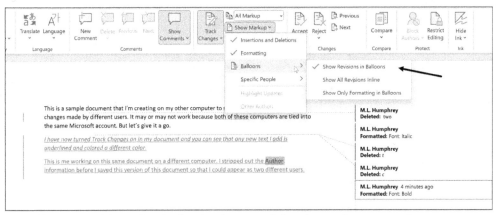

The nice thing about this setting is that it takes out deleted text from your document so you still can see changes in the document but you don't have to mentally remove the deleted text. See the Track Changes example there in the second paragraph as an example of how that works.

Show revisions inline basically is what you saw above with the All Markup screenshot, but this time there's no note off to the side to call-out the formatting changes. They're just there with no specific mention that they were made. (So not a setting I personally like to use.)

Finally, you can choose to only see edits from specific people if you want. Again, personally, not something I would do because I was always looking at the entirety of the document and whether the entire thing worked as a final report. But I'm sure there are times when it makes sense to hide the edits made by one specific user. For example, maybe if an analyst reformatted the document with track changes on and you don't want those changes flagged during your review.

Advanced Options

You can customize track changes by clicking on the expansion arrow in the Tracking section of the Review tab to open the Track Changes Options dialogue box:

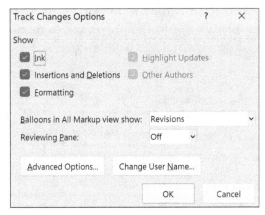

That allows you to then click on Advanced Options to open the Advanced Track Changes Options dialogue box:

This is where you can change the colors used for tracking changes as well as how tracked changes are shown in the document. So you could set it so that there is just one color used for all changes regardless of the author and you could even choose what that color is.

I want to say back in the day legal documents used a double black-line strikethrough for deletions, for example. This is where you could set your document to do that.

Just know that this is a personal setting that will apply for your version of the document, but not for someone else looking at the same document.

Okay, now that we've covered all of the appearance settings, time to actually review the changes and accept them or reject them.

Review Changes

To review the changes in your document, you can turn on the Reviewing Pane and scroll through that way, but what I prefer is to either read the document or, if there are scattered or small changes, use the Previous and Next options in the Changes section of the Review tab:

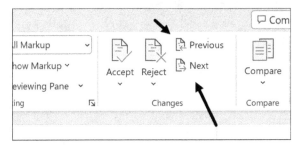

Click on Next to move forward to the next change in the document. Word will move through the document, find the next change, and highlight it. Click on Previous to move backward through the document.

Accept or Reject Changes

In that same section, you have the option to Accept or Reject. Both of those have a dropdown menu with a variety of choices.

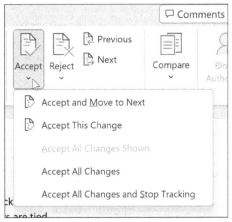

Here you can see that for Accept the options are to accept and move to next, accept this change, accept all changes, or accept all changes and stop tracking.

I tend not to accept or reject a single change at a time. And the reason for that is what you can see with that track changes edit. Word considers that six separate changes. First was the addition of track and changes, then was the deletion of the lower-case t and c, and then was the addition of the upper-case t and c.

Rather than walk through those six changes and accept them individually, what I do is select both words and then click on Accept. That accepts all six changes at once.

So usually I walk through a document using previous and next, read that phrase, sentence, or paragraph, make any additional edits I think are needed and then select the whole thing and accept the edits. (Assuming this is a final pass that no one else needs to review. Obviously, don't accept all changes if someone needs to see what you did.)

Turn Off Track Changes

When you are done with your document and all changes have been made and accepted, turn off track changes. Yes, I have said this ten times. I probably need to say it ten more. DO NOT leave track changes turned on in your document. One, it's a nuisance if you then go to make any edit whatsoever to the document. And, two, you do not want to run the risk of circulating a "final" document that actually has a bunch of tracked changes in it.

When track changes is on, your status in the top right corner will be Reviewing and when it is off your status will be Editing.

Final Document Review

Before you finalize your document, you can have Word review the document for any lingering tracked changes that weren't accepted or rejected.

To do so, go to the File tab and then click on Info. There is an option there to Inspect Document. Click on Check for Issues to see if there are still tracked changes present in the document:

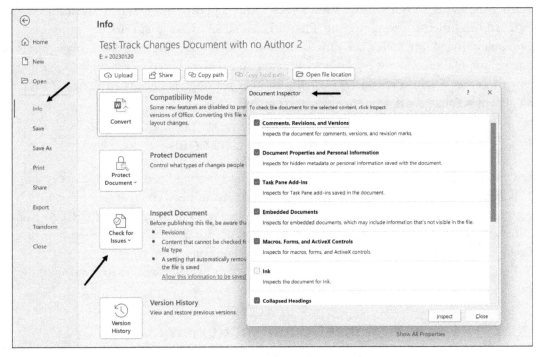

It will be part of the Comments, Revisions, and Versions option.

(Just be careful about removing your document properties and personal information, which I warned about above. That is under Document Properties and Personal Information.)

Comments

For me, comments in Word go hand-in-hand with track changes, but they're actually two separate things, so I've separated them into two separate chapters. Here is an example of a comment and the beginning of a response:

You can see that by default comments are visible off to the side of the main text and that the document will have a little comment bubble there to the right of the text to indicate the existence of a comment.

I left the response unfinished so you could also see that tip that says to use Ctrl + Enter to post a response. If you just use Enter, it goes to a new line within the comment. Your other option for finalizing a comment is to click on that blue button with the arrow in it.

Here is what it looks like when someone has made a comment and then someone else has responded to that comment:

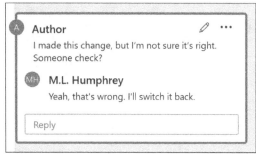

To edit a response, just hold your cursor over it and you'll see the pencil appear next to the name of the person who commented. Click on that and then make your changes.

One fault in Word is that you can actually edit someone else's comment. So I can click on that little pencil in the top right corner of the comment box and edit the comment made by Author even though I'm currently M.L. Humphrey to Word.

Alright. So how do you add a comment in the first place?

Place your cursor at the location in the document where you want to make a comment and then go to the Comments section of the Review tab and click on New Comment:

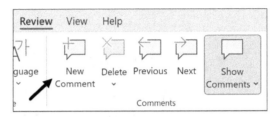

You can also use Ctrl + Alt + M or right-click and choose New Comment from the dropdown menu. When you click on that option, Word will insert a new comment window with the cursor in the beginning of the comment window. You can either type your text and then use Ctrl + Enter or the button with the blue arrow to add that comment or click on the X if you changed your mind.

While a comment is selected, Word shifts it to the left like you can see below with the middle comment.

When no comments are selected they all align.

The Delete option in the Comments section will let you delete the current comment, delete all comments in the document, or delete all resolved comments. You can also click on an individual comment and then right-click on the … in the top right corner and choose Delete Thread to delete a comment and any responses.

To Resolve a comment, right-click on the … in the top right corner of the comment and then choose to Resolve Thread:

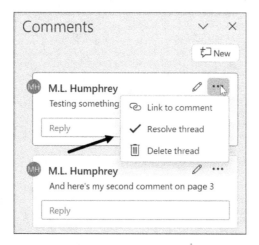

The comment will be marked as Resolved and grayed out, but will still appear in your document:

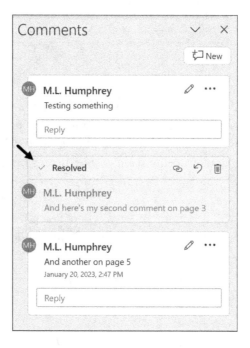

This option is not available if you are in Compatibility Mode, so have opened a .doc file instead of a .docx file.

The Show Comments dropdown in the Comments section has two options, Contextual or List. Contextual places the comments next to where they were made in the document. List shows all comments from the document in a Comments task pane:

The comments are all listed together regardless of what page they appear on. Above, for example, there were comments I made on page 1, page 3, and page 5. Even when I scroll to page 7, all three of those comments are listed in that task pane. Whereas with the Contextual option they only show when you're on the page where the comment was made.

If you are in the List view, you can click on a comment to go to the page that contains that comment.

You can make comments on a document even when Track Changes are turned off.

If you have track changes in a document that display in a balloon off to the right side, any comments will be pushed to the right of those tracked changes and may not be readily visible.

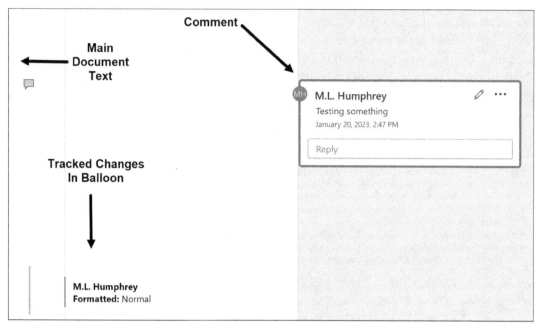

You can fix this by setting tracked changes to display inline.

Another option is to click on the Comments button in the top right corner of the workspace to open the Comments task pane to see the text of your comments, but that task pane will appear on top of any tracked changes balloons. If you close the Navigation task pane, however, then you can have the Comments task pane visible as well as any tracked changes shown in balloons.

You can use the Previous and Next options in the Comments section of the Review tab to move through the comments in your document.

However, Word will skip any comments that have been marked as resolved. Furthermore, it will not show those comments off to the side with your active comments. They will only be indicated by the comment icon to the right of your text.

Here is one open comment with the comment displayed and then you can see the comment bubble for a resolve comment below that:

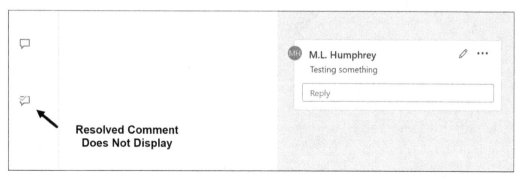

You can still see the resolved comment by clicking on that comment bubble.

Also, you cannot make a comment directly on a footnote or endnote. (That would be very nice to have Microsoft people, if you're looking for things you can do to improve the program.)

If you're used to how comments worked previously in Word, including with a dotted line between the comment and text it was addressing, you can currently revert back to the old way of doing things by going to the File tab and then Options and the General page and unchecking the box for Enable Modern Comments.

Here's how that used to look with a dotted line between the comment and where in the document someone was trying to place that comment:

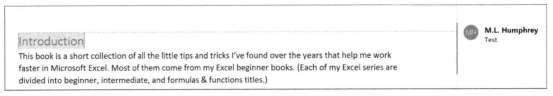

They are going to retire the ability to switch back at some point, but for now it's still an option. You may have to close Word and reopen before that change takes effect, though.

Compare Documents

The final aspect to track changes and comments is comparing documents. I mentioned it before, because it's the most sure-fire way to know that you're seeing all changes that were made to a document. You take the original document, you take the new document, and you give them both to Word and tell it to flag any changes.

But it can also be a bit messy at times especially if text was moved around. Still, it's nice to know about if you need it.

First step, open a new document in Word. Go to the Review tab and find the Compare dropdown in the Compare section on the right-hand side. Click on Compare.

The Compare Documents dialogue box will appear:

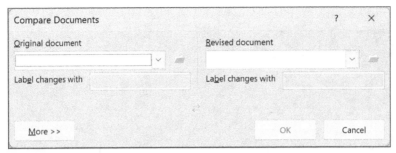

The left-hand side is the original of the document. The right-hand side is the updated version. Click on the dropdown menu to see recent documents you've used and select one of those files or use the little folder to the right of the dropdown to go find your file.

Word will automatically populate the Label Changes With field with a user name, but you can change that if you want.

Click on More to tell Word which changes to identify and how to treat changes like the one we talked about before with "track changes" being changed to "Track Changes".

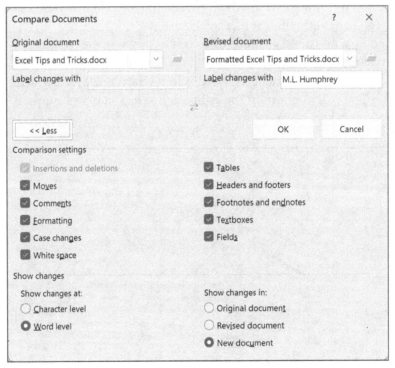

If you choose to show changes at the character level then it will look like the example from above. If you choose to show at the word level it will show that as a deletion of track changes replaced with an insertion of Track Changes instead of just changes to the individual letters.

You can also choose whether to show those changes in the original document, the revised document, or a new document. The default is new document which is what I always choose as well.

Click on OK when you're done. Here we go:

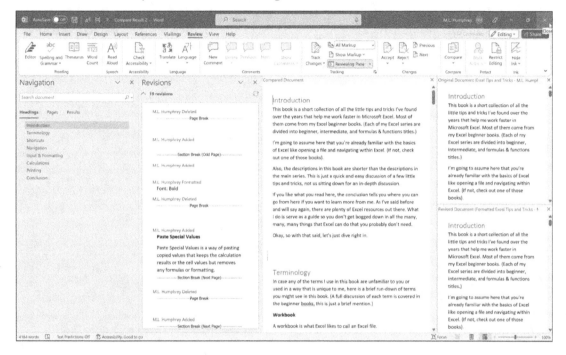

That looks chaotic, but we can hide the Navigation pane and that leaves me with a Revisions pane on the left-hand side, the new document in the center and then the original document on the top right and the revised document on the bottom right.

Click on an edit in the Revisions pane to go to that section of the other documents:

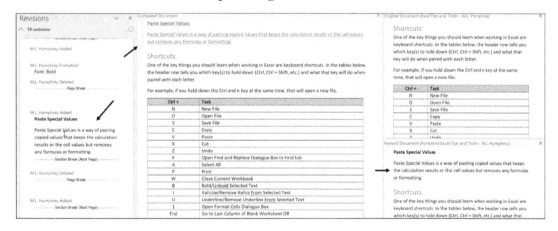

You can see above, for example, a change I made where I added text related to Paste Special Values within the document. Word recorded that as adding text. You can see it reflected as a tracked change in the new document, see that that text was not in the original, and see that text in the revised document.

I often find with document compare that I just want to view the new comparison document. You can do that by clicking on the X in the corner of the original and revised documents to close them.

That also makes the page breaks in the new comparison document appear, which helps me understand what this particular change was:

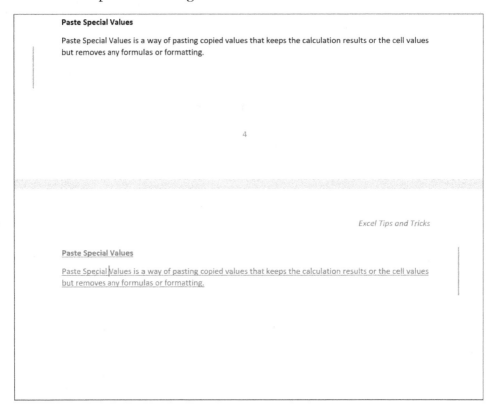

Now I can see (and remember) that what I did here was copy text from the end of that chapter and paste it in there so that I would force the chapter start to the next page. I did that so I could demonstrate a specific type of section break. The fact that the text was not part of the next chapter was not obvious if you look at the screenshot above this one because Word in that view was not showing page and section breaks on the screen.

But you can see that what I ended up with was a document that has track changes that reflect formatting changes, the addition/deletion of page and section breaks, and the addition of headers and footers as well.

Usually I only need this when a document was edited but not in track changes. I have also used it when someone edited a document and some of the changes I made to their edits were to reject additions or deletions they made, which you can't see in track changes at the end.

So what I did in that situation is accepted all changes in their version and then compared that document to my final version after I had accepted or rejected their changes. That left me with a document where the only track changes in the document were edits on their edits.

Okay. We're getting towards the end, but let's quickly cover footnotes and endnotes and then maybe a few tiny items.

Footnotes and Endnotes

Footnotes and Endnotes can both be added to a document from the Footnotes section of the References tab. The main option there is to Insert Footnote but there is also an option to Insert Endnote.

Click at the point you want to insert your note and then click on the option you want to use. Word will automatically insert the note on that page (for a footnote) or at the end of the document (for an endnote). The note will be below a line and will have a superscript number both at the point of insertion and in that footnote or endnote section:

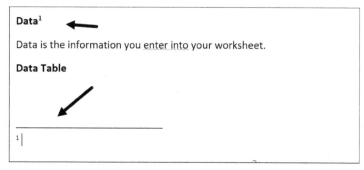

Type whatever text you want to type for the note and then click back into the main document.

You can see the text of a note you've added to your document at that point in the document by holding your mouse over the number:

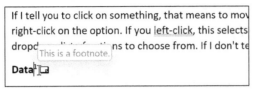

Here I have my mouse over the 1 next to Data and I can see the text "This is a footnote" that I added as my footnote.

To delete a footnote or endnote, just delete that number from within your text.

If you want to convert a footnote to an endnote or vice versa, right-click on the note and choose the Convert to [X] option from the dropdown menu.

There is also a Note Options choice in the dropdown menu. Click on that to open the Footnote and Endnote dialogue box:

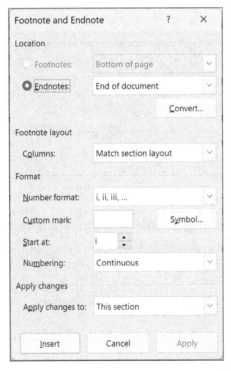

This allows you to choose the numbering style and formatting of the notes in your document.

If you need to navigate between the footnotes or endnotes in your document, the Footnotes section of the References tab has a dropdown under Next Footnote that allows you to either go to the next footnote, previous footnote, next endnote, or previous endnote in the document.

Miscellaneous Topics

Real quick I'm going to mention a few topics we're not covering in detail here.

Insert Citations, Captions, or Index Entries

The References tab also has options for inserting citations, captions, index entries, or a table of authorities.

Dictation

Word does have a dictation option in the Voice section of the Home tab.

Hyperlink

If you need to provide a website link, you can use the Link option in the Links section of the Insert tab. This also lets you link to other documents, other locations within the document, or to an email address.

Word Themes

If you don't like the default Word theme, there are a number of additional choices on the Design tab.

Line Numbering

You can add line numbering from the Page Setup section of the Layout tab.

Hyphenation

You can hyphenate the text in your paragraphs from the Page Setup section of the Layout tab.

Mail Merge

You can create mail merge documents using the Mailings tab. This usually requires integration with an Excel spreadsheet that has your list of recipients and their related information.

Read Aloud

You can have Word read your document aloud to you using the Read Aloud option in the Speech section of the Review tab. Note that the voice it uses if you are offline is much less natural sounding than the one it uses if you are online, at least by default.

Online Collaboration

It is possible to have multiple people editing the same document at the same time using online collaboration tools in Word. (I personally think that's a nightmare scenario, but I do know author teams who use it.)

Sort

If you ever have a list of entries that you need to sort alphabetically, you can do so using the Sort option in the Paragraph section of the Home tab which shows an A on top of a Z with a downpointing arrow.

You can use this with tables but I also have used it in the past with a list of text entries that I wanted to alphabetize quickly. As long as they're on separate lines, they're easy to sort.

Conclusion

Alright. That was *Intermediate Word 365*. It was not everything you can do in Word. As you can see from that last chapter, there are a good dozen topics right there that I could have covered in another forty pages or so that I chose to only mention. And there are other things you can do in Word that I didn't mention at all, like everything covered in the Draw tab.

The service I provide with these books is giving you a path through the wide variety of things you can do in Word so that you don't get lost while trying to learn what you need to learn. But it is entirely possible that I did not cover something you need to know, like mail merges.

The first step when there's something you want to learn about in Word is to, if you know where it is already, hold your mouse over that option:

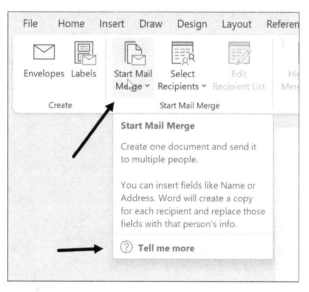

Often there will be a Tell Me More link at the bottom of the basic description that Word gives for that task. Click on that option and Word's help task pane will open to a help topic specific to that task.

If that isn't available, you can go to the Help tab and click on one of the help options there. F1 will also open the Help task pane. You have to be online to use Word's help these days but it is very helpful.

Another option if that doesn't work is a web search for your topic combined with the words "Word 365" or "Microsoft Office Word" and then whatever it is you're trying to learn about.

Microsoft's help is generally very good for how something works. They're less helpful when it comes to "is this possible" type questions. But the internet is vast and somewhere out there it is very likely that someone has already provided the answer to your question if you just look for it. Sometimes knowing what to search for is a bit tricky if you don't know the terms, but 9 times out of 10 or more like 999 out of 1000 the answer is out there.

For example, when I was writing this book and my columns weren't evening out I thought, "that should be possible, shouldn't it?" so I did an internet search and found a website that had told how to do it back in 2006. Perfect.

And if you ever have confusion about anything I covered here or just want to ask me about something, reach out. I'm happy to help. I can't guarantee an immediate response, but I usually will see an email and respond within a few days.

Okay, then. Good luck with it. Don't be afraid to experiment. Ctrl + Z, Undo, is your friend. And remember that sometimes if a document with really complex formatting starts doing strange things to you, the best bet is to strip all of that formatting out and start over, as painful as that thought might be.

Index

About the Author

M.L. Humphrey is a former stockbroker with a degree in Economics from Stanford and an MBA from Wharton who has spent close to twenty years as a regulator and consultant in the financial services industry.

You can reach M.L. at mlhumphreywriter@gmail.com or at mlhumphrey.com.

www.ingramcontent.com/pod-product-compliance
Lightning Source LLC
LaVergne TN
LVHW081339050326
832903LV00024B/1217